PEACEABLE NATURE

Peaceable Nature

An Optimistic View of Life on Earth

STEPHAN LACKNER

1817

Harper & Row, Publishers, San Francisco

Cambridge, Hagerstown, New York, Philadelphia
London, Mexico City, São Paulo, Singapore, Sydney

This English-language edition of *Peaceable Nature* constitutes a translation and revision of the original German edition of the book published under the title *Die friedfertige Natur* by Kösel-Verlag, Munich. Copyright © 1982 Kösel-Verlag GmbH & Co., München.

FIRST EDITION

Library of Congress Cataloging in Publication Data
Lackner, Stephan.
    PEACEABLE NATURE.
    Translation and revision of: Die friedfertige Natur.
    1. Philosophy of nature. 2. Biology—Philosophy.
    3. Philosophical anthropology.   I. Title.
BD581.L1813 1984   113   83-48985
ISBN 0-06-250489-4

84 85 86 87 88 10 9 8 7 6 5 4 3 2 1

To my beloved wife

Contents

Introduction:
Biosophy—A New Orientation

Peace, the most urgent business of our time, does not find any support from the traditional thinking of most biologists. Neo-Darwinism maintains that struggle is not only prevalent everywhere in nature, but that combat is beneficial for the vigorous development of species.

Forceable selection of the fittest through the struggle for survival: This has been the basic dogma of biology for more than 120 years. From this cruel premise all essential phenomena are deduced: the improvement of life forms, the ranking order among unrelated varieties of animals, industrial progress, and even the purpose of life. When the old-fashioned Darwinian scientist gazes into a golden-green landscape, he probably feels guilty neglecting to find combat or at least competition out there.

Yet, as Darwin well knew, the fauna of numerous predatorless islands has been thriving without degenerating through millennia. Millions of flamingos lead a most peaceable life, safe from all enemies as they wade in shallow African lakes. Yet peaceful habitats are considered exceptions. The "real world," for the neo-Darwinist, is filled with unrelenting competition, meting out destruction to all weak, deformed, and "unfit" creatures.

But are animals that never kill and are never killed unfit for life?

Nature is incredibly more diversified than the mechanical rule "survival of the fittest" would lead us to expect. Nature has always, almost playfully, produced innumerable fantastic forms, many of which have remained stable and efficient. Love, cooperation, and symbiosis have been at work on this morphological richness at least as much as competition.

If the Darwinian principles of elimination were really almighty, the earth would be populated with drably camouflaged, prickly, evil-tasting, and poisonous beings. This is obviously not the case. With radiant flowers and sweet birdsong, with peacocks and butterflies, beauty has spread throughout the biosphere. This means that there must be other laws which counteract the rigidity of an all-pervasive struggle for life.

Some biologists maintain that natural death should indeed be called "unnatural." This can easily be disproved. After long years of study and observation, I have become convinced that about 95 percent of all beings lead peaceful lives, dying when their biological clocks have run down. This rule, of course, is valid only when and where the rapaciousness of homo sapiens has not interfered.

The notion of basic aggressiveness is needed by certain naturalists as an important building block for their theoretical system. This requirement leads to quite horrifying pronouncements, such as Edward O. Wilson's: "Are human beings innately aggressive? . . . The answer is yes."[1] Or Robert Ardrey's: "Man is a predator with a natural instinct to kill with a weapon."[2]

Certainly, cruelty and violence are effective in the animal kingdom and have contributed to the great adventure of evolution. This we can admit, but without enthusiasm.

A peacefully oriented biology would give humanity some new grounds for optimism. It would help to show that creatures everywhere regard life as a desirable good and not as a prelude to castastrophe. Most young mammals, while at play, seem personifications of *joie de vivre*. The blossom turns toward the sun, and the butterfly enjoys its nectar. Sex usually means rapture.

Now if life itself is a positive good, we don't have to search for transcendental meanings and superimposed purposes for an average earthly life. Then we can live for life's sake. Thus Heinrich Heine wrote to Karl Gutzkow, on August 28, 1838: "Art is the purpose of art, just as love is the purpose of love and, indeed, life itself is the purpose of life."

Quite a number of open-minded younger biologists are coming

around to the idea of a "soft biology." But the traditional, Darwin-encrusted life scientists probably won't revise the foundations of their system very soon. It might be easier and more advantageous to subsume new trends and unorthodox ideas under a new concept. "Biosophy," the wisdom of life, can counteract the dreary fatalism of existentialists and behaviorists, and give us desperately needed hope. Life simply is not *bellum omnium contra omnes*, "war of all against all."

Darwin's original concept of evolution through natural selection was a stroke of genius. Yet selection in nature takes place not only by dint of struggle and combat, but also through symbiotic arrangement and, in higher-organized animals, through loving choice of partners. This is the point where biosophy, though beholden to Darwin, has to part company with neo-Darwinism.

A biosophical overview has ramifications in many fields and pursuits of knowledge, from paleontology to historiography to futurology and practical help in living. Biosophy shows that we do not act naturally when proclaiming war as the basic law of existence on this lovely planet. The warrior acts against nature.

Biosophy, as a hybrid of biology and philosophy, should combine detailed investigation with the philosophical will to generalize. No sectarian divergence is intended. But certain modern tendencies could converge under this title and thereby become more effective.

The problems of aggression have haunted me since I was an American soldier in World War II, fighting against Germany, my former homeland. I came to regard the large-scale destruction around me as counterproductive. As everybody agrees by now, the senselessness of war is mounting. The Stockholm Peace Institute has established that in World War I, 20 percent of the victims were civilians, in World War II more than half were civilians; and in the Vietnam War 90 percent of those killed were non-military persons. A linear projection of this curve would engulf us all.

When Dr. Samuel T. Cohen, the "father of the neutron bomb," was interviewed on Dutch television in 1981, he was asked: "Do you think there will be war?" "Yes," was Cohen's answer, "it's terrible to say. Yes, I think so. I think that fighting is simply human nature. There always were wars."

The dogma that the aggressive drive is inherited in the genes of every human being is contradicted by many anthropological observations. The example of the pacific Hunza in Asia has become famous. The small Semai tribe in Malaysia, left to its own devices, also knows no aggression. Children there are never chastised bodily, they never witness the use of compulsion, and hence cannot imitate any violent behavior. Murder is unknown among the Semai. True, some of the most peaceful tribes were whipped into a frenzy of bloodthirstiness while menaced by the Japanese "co-prosperity sphere" or, as in Malaya in the 1950s, by Communist guerillas. But this proves clearly that aggressiveness is an acquired, not an inherited, character trait.

My deepest hope is that this book will further the pacification of our species by showing that peace is not something contrived and exceptional. We humans have only to yield to—mostly peaceable —nature.

1. Nature—How Red in Tooth and Claw?

"It is getting dark," said the mayfly,
"the world's only day is ending."

Who knows? Perhaps solutions to our disquieting problems are somewhere on the billions of printed pages, just waiting to be recognized. Sometimes the most pretentious summations of a philosophy are rather platitudinous or downright false. And sometimes an inconspicuous remark may open up the most unexpected vistas. One such modest sentence, which seems to me of inestimable significance, was written by Goethe to Heinrich Meyer in a letter of August 8, 1792: "The purpose of life is life itself—and when we have done our share inwardly, the outer things will follow of themselves."

This insight is still unsurpassed.

Following Goethe's lead, we arrive at the doctrine of *life for life's sake*. This formula, with its implications and ramifications, comprises all that is dear to the heart of undogmatic, liberal, modern people. With joy and pain, with lust and renouncement, with shimmering surprises and sticky boredom, with guilt and forgetfulness, with *angst* and glory: This is your only life and, therefore, it is immensely important to you.

To live for life itself: This challenge makes sense only if life is directed toward certain desirable aims. Otherwise, it would be a vicious circle, like the mythical scorpion who kills itself with its own tail stinger. If life would be "war of all against all"—implying also war against ourselves—then it would not be worthwhile; such a dreary existence could not possibly challenge normal human beings to high efforts and sacrifices.

"Dog eats dog," the "realist" shrugs. But how often has any of us actually seen this?

Suppression of the weaker in a pitiless pecking order, reinforcement of hierarchic structures, unquestioning adherence to "impartial" laws favoring acquisitive characters, might makes right—those were the lessons late nineteenth-century natural science offered to a greedy industrial-imperialist society, and which denatured the Victorian epoch's *joie-de-vivre*.

Yet life is not hierarchical. Life surrounds our planet as a functional web. It consists as much of cooperation as of competition. It is not by going against nature's tendencies, but by integrating ourselves into the great tapestry of flora and fauna that we can conceive and realize our most human ideals.

Even an adult male chimpanzee will voluntarily hand a scrap of meat to a supplicant, to a weak young chimp whose gestures say "pretty please." Altruism, if not exactly prevalent, at least occurs in the primeval forests.

I believe that the most advanced biological research will lead to biosophical conclusions. Using sophisticated biochemistry and computer wizardry, some biologists have already found that in the early stages of life, symbiosis was the major evolutionary process.

This view, however, has not yet filtered down into the writings of popularizers. Let me, therefore, quote from a pertinent article by the New Zealand scientist, G. A. M. King:

The idea of symbiosis (from Greek "sumbioein," meaning "to live together") has been interpreted in a wide variety of ways. We shall apply it to the physical union between members of associating species which leads to a propagating species. A common example is a lichen, formed by the union of a fungus and an alga. . . . One crucial step in the evolution of higher life, the step from the prokaryotic cell to the eukaryotic, has been attributed to a series of symbioses. Indeed, it is now commonly recognised that the chloroplast found in plant cells evolved from the symbiotic inclusion of a blue-green alga into a primitive eukaryotic cell. . . . Many chloroplastic proteins and almost all mitochondrial proteins are encoded on the nuclear DNA. If the symbiotic origin of these organelles is accepted, it is necessary to accept at the same time that the symbioses have been consolidated by mutation in the nuclear DNA. . . .[3]

These scientific findings contradict the hallowed neo-Darwinian dogma that only random, accidental mutations can modify the genetic heritage of organisms. The mystique of the chromosome has been broken: Environment can indeed influence genes. Chlorophyll has originally been utilized by including living blue-green algae in the cells of different plants, thus making photosynthesis the viable basis of the entire food chain. Thus symbiosis was and is the central phenomenon of all life.

Cooperation in nature is at least as frequent and decisive as competition. In order to gain this higher perspective, we only have to view the superimposed structures of life. A lawn is obviously a unit—it wants to spread and maintain its own well-being, it overgrows its bald spots, it heals its wounds like any organism. A lake reacts to poisoning as a body does, additions of fresh water and nourishment benefit the whole, the rapacity and symbiosis of its inhabitants form an everrenewed equilibrium. There are sick and healthy ponds and streams, just as there are sickly and vigorous individuals.

It is not only possible but advantageous to extend this "soft" biology to other living phenomena. A field of wheat exists through visible acts of brotherliness: No single stalk could defend itself against wind and weather. In our purposeful endeavor, we have enhanced this natural helpfulness through breeding. Each wheat plant relies on its neighbors for support; otherwise it would have to divert much of its life-energy to producing more cellulose and siliceous components, to stiffen its stalk, and it would not produce big, succulent grains. In this case, cooperation is better for the economy than competition. The wheat field shows very clearly that it is not the most egotistical individual who is most successful, but the most cooperative one.

Why not pursue this principle to a better understanding of other forms of life? A forest, for example, often behaves like one superorganism. The fringe of the forest turns a thick, almost impenetrable front of interwoven branches toward the open surroundings. The trees at the edge are endowed with green branches from top to bottom; their construction differs from the bald, high trunks in the forest's interior, just as skin cells differ from muscle and bone cells. The forest's mantle is an organ, comparable to our skin. It protects the interior from storms, violent temperature changes, and desiccation; it also protects the insect-eating birds, which are necessary for the ecological balance. Together with the dense roof of the tree tops, the mantle also prevents overpopulation. If all seeds and seedlings were allowed to grow to maturity, the entire forest would suffocate. Of course, the well-being of the forest is more important than the potential lives of its seeds. By shutting out the light supply from the interior, the forest has developed a most effective method of birth control. It is high time that humanity thinks of itself as one functional unit, comparable to meadow and forest, and acts accordingly.

This natural population control has to be viewed not as a cruel form of competition, but as part of the overall process of cooperation. It does not give us a scientific justification to designate the "struggle for life" as the overriding principle. We don't think it cruel that millions of spermatozoa perish so that one of them can succeed in fertilizing an ovum. Likewise, we should not regret the elimination of surplus seeds, seedlings, tiny fish: An overly fertile species must relieve the crowding of its adult members and maintain its optimum number.

We must consider the web of life as a functional garment surrounding our planet. Its *gestalt* is more decisive than its single components.

Botanists have produced almost miraculous improvements in fruit-bearing plants. In helping to feed a hungry world, they have also helped these plants to come into a healthier existence in ever-increasing numbers. It won't be possible to breed better people by the same methods, though, because we will never agree which particular features should be considered desirable. There have been attempts at "ennobling" the human race, of course, the most prominent and disastrous being the German *Lebensborne* of the SS. The medieval *jus primae noctis,* the right of aristocratic masters to deflower their subjects' brides, and the plantation owners' privilege to sleep with their female slaves were founded on the same *hubris.* It would, however, be desirable for our educators and philosophers to strengthen a type of human being who, like the single stalk in a wheat field, can trustingly lean on his or her neighbors and thereby convert more vital energy into fruitful and enjoyable activities.

Cooperation is not the exception, but the natural rule. Without superimposed ecosystems there is no singular life. Without the microbes in the soil, without earthworms and ants plowing up and always redigesting the topsoil, no meadows and forests could exist. Without bacteria to digest the input in our digestive tracts, the output of science and poetry would not be possible. Propagation and cadaver-disposal—the beginning and the end of every individual life—can only take place cooperatively.

We must accommodate our thinking to this view; we must consider communities, woods and ponds, even continents and oceans, as breathing entities. Then we will feel a certain readiness to accept selective principles for the sake of ecological equilibrium. Birth control will seem not a cruel manipulation, but a natural tendency. And wars, which eliminate the best and the most useful, will appear unnatural.

Does life equal strife?

Glancing over the panorama of life, we find more exceptions than confirmations of this cruel dogma. The largest mammals are vegetarians—they don't eat other animals. The elephant, rhino, and hippopotamus are too imposing to be attacked by predators; and they invest so much of their living substance into thick skins that they are virtually impervious to small meat-eaters, snakes, and parasites. Before the appearance of man these giants had no enemies. Much the same holds true for certain whales, vultures, and giant turtles.

On the other end of the scale, countless flying insects such as gnats and ephemerae are too tiny to be much of a meal. A few are eaten by hummingbirds and spiders, but the overwhelming majority of mayflies die peacefully in the evening, when their biological clocks have run down.

The so-called "law of the jungle," which yields every right to the mighty, seems to be a fantasy of the age of colonialism to justify war, slavery, and oppression. In recent decades, observations of dedicated naturalists have given us a much more peaceful picture of jungle life. Even the gorilla, once feared as the embodiment of dimwitted aggressiveness, has proved to be a shy, sensitive creature. Our aboriginal fear of jungle and rainforest should by now be reversed—it is our own greed for wood and building sites that menaces the primitive forests and their inhabitants.

It is extremely difficult to estimate how many jungle animals die of violence. In open grazing country, however, the ratio of predator to potential prey can be more easily ascertained. We have found that the percentage of these creatures killed in a bloody fashion is surprisingly small, compared with those that die from "natural" causes.

The enormous herds of buffalo that populated the North American plains through millennia knew hardly any enemies. Wolf, puma, and bear, surveying the outer fringes, could not harm the vital adult buffalo; the predators had to be content with sick and aged specimens. The Indians took possibly one-hundred-thousandth of a herd each year—only enough to meet their needs. It was the white man, wanting to deprive the hated "redskins" of their ecological basis for survival, who virtually exterminated the buffalo.

The ratio of predators to vegetarians has been established in some African wildlife preserves. The Serengeti Park contains about 500,000 wildebeests, 180,000 Thomson's gazelles, 150,000 zebras, 65,000 impalas, 50,000 buffalos, and thousands of other gazelles and giraffes. It is the largest and most concentrated collection of hoofed animals on earth. They lead a relaxed life, grazing, resting, and wandering about without paying much attention to the predators that exist among them. The flight instinct takes hold of only small groups of the total herd at a time, depending on distance, mood, and movements of the hunters. Each burst of panic ends quickly, and peace prevails again.

Aggressors that make their living as meat-eaters include lions, hyenas, wild dogs, and cheetahs. Every lion requires, on the average, fourteen to twenty pounds of meat a day. It was observed that a pride of two males, three females, and eight cubs disposed of four wildebeests within thirteen days. Perhaps twenty to thirty victims are killed by one lion per year. All the lions of the Serengeti together may kill 40,000 to 72,000 hoofed animals—less than 7 percent of the million vegetarians at their disposal. The hyenas of the same habitat kill probably 30,000 victims, the other meat-eaters a few thousand more. Competent observers such as George Schaller and Hans Kruuk indicate that less than 10 percent of the grazing animals die of violence.[4]

If we take into account that each carcass feeds not only the hunter and its companions and young ones, but also vultures, jackals, insects, worms and, finally, the plants that take over the remains, the ratio of violent to peaceful deaths becomes minimal indeed.

Relations among the large mammals of northern climes are not much different. Wolves and deer tend to maintain a steady ecological equilibrium—except when there is human interference, of course. A 140-pound male wolf, his 80-pound mate, and two 60-pound cubs together eat about 140 pounds of meat per week. This means that one killed deer satisfies four wolves so that they won't hunt anything else for a week. In the Rocky Mountains, a single puma used to exert the same population control as four wolves. Lynx, wildcat, coyote, fox, and some Indians also used to find their steady livelihood from deer, supplemented by squirrels and other rodents. In turn, this mild reduction of the vegetarians' number helped to stabilize plant growth. That original ecosystem has now been widely destroyed.

Due to several lucky coincidences the vital equilibrium on Isle Royale in Lake Superior has been reinstated, and there David Mech has ascertained to what extent nature can be called "red in tooth and claw." This island is now protected by the U.S. Park Service as a primitive region. At the beginning of the twentieth century a herd of moose wandered from Canada across the ice and established itself on Isle Royale. Lacking enemies, it grew to 3000 head. In 1949 Canadian wolves crossed the ice, reducing the herd to between 600 and 1000 animals. The number of wolves remains constant at 20 to 25. They have to work quite strenuously to kill one moose—mainly very young, very old, or sick individuals—every third day. Wolves, moose, and vegetation complement each others' existence. The average number of births equals the number of deaths. To call nature "cruel" in this comfortable niche would be nonsensical.

On numerous other islands—on the Galapagos, for example, where giant tortoises and finches had no enemies and developed beautifully—the conditions were even more auspicious for serene life cycles. These and other peaceful enclaves prove that predators are simply not needed to enforce vigorous health and genetic improvement of populations. On Hawaii, for untold centuries, there existed only those animals that had winged their way across the wide ocean—namely, insects and birds. There was only a single predator, an owl. Human traffic upset this paradisiacal equilibrium by introducing a rapacious fauna.

Pursuing our panorama of animal life we find that, among all creatures, rodents, small fish, and certain insects are eaten in the largest quantities. These different life forms have invented the same strategy for survival of their species: uninhibited multiplication. The populations of many rodents and winged insects exist in instable, always changing, always endangered balance. If their numbers are not constantly held in check, if predaceous enemies become inefficient, if weather and vegetation growth become too favorable, the results are overwhelming plagues of locusts, mice, rats, or caterpillars.

Nature has usually provided more efficacious resistors within these cycles than has our chemistry, with its tendency to overkill. Spiders and bats, frogs and hedgehogs take care of many of those insects we consider noxious. Birds have also done their part: Blue titmice have been observed carrying food to their nestlings 475 times a day. A pair of song thrush caught 336 larvae and winged insects every average day, and robins near Oxford visited their fledglings 27 times every hour, providing two or three caterpillars on each trip.

Certainly not all birds have this murderous efficiency. Many species eat only grains and berries. And berries don't mind, they actually demand to be eaten and thus distributed to faraway places with the birds' excrements. That is their life-allotted task.

If we look at the other side of the coin, we find that adult birds themselves are not eaten as frequently as mice or fish. Falcons, owls, and cats take their share, but the numbers are relatively small and hardly amount to population control. Out of the huge penguin flocks only the sea leopard, a very aggressive seal, manages to snap an occasional victim; otherwise, the adult penguins have no enemies. The hundreds of thousands of flamingos wading in shallow African lakes suffer no persecution whatsoever. But it happens, albeit rarely, that a careless flamingo venturing on shore is caught by a jackal or a hyena. One in a million!

I don't want to count eggs among the victims of aggression because they don't experience fear or pain. However, we feel pity for fledglings eaten before their time, and in the fledgling stage bird populations are indeed decimated quite cruelly. This does not alter the fact that many bird species never fall prey to other animals. Swallows, swifts, swans, and storks are largely invulnerable; it seems to help a bird to begin its name with an "s." Most birds die of exhaustion and hunger, cold, sickness, and old age, without having their blood shed by some tooth or claw.

Reptiles, on the other hand, happen to need only small quantities of food. They don't have to heat their bodies, and they remain immobile when they are cold; thus their metabolism requires little fuel. The boa constrictor likes to swallow one whole pig, after which it does not have to eat again for almost a year!

Turning to the amphibians, we can see clearly that their numerically overwhelming propagation is only a defensive reaction to the rapaciousness of predators. Where these animals don't run the risk of overpopulation in order to maintain their numbers in the face of gluttonous enemies, they develop some mysterious birth-control schemes. Animals that are poisonous, evil-smelling, or bitter-tasting—and hence not eaten very often—simply don't produce large quantities of descendents. This becomes very obvious when various kinds of frogs are compared. In Costa Rica's rainforest lives the poison-arrow frog. The poisonous adults, who advertise this fact with garish colors, are never bothered by even the hungriest enemies. The female, who has discovered the trick of laying her eggs into a rolled-up leaf where they are protected from the eyes of thieves, only needs to produce five eggs. Other kinds of frogs in the same region deposit their egg masses openly on the faces of leaves, where they are devoured by snakes. Consequently, each female leaf frog produces hundreds of eggs to compensate for the loss.

In the course of evolution, species that brought forth too little spawn or too few litters or did not institute protective measures for their offspring simply died out. This selective pressure caused toads to lay thousands of eggs each, whereas the female newt, which folds leaves in such an artful way that her eggs remain glued into a protective sheath until they hatch, produces less than a hundred. These observations contradict the thesis of sociobiology that all living organisms have one aim, namely, to produce as many descendants as possible.

Fish are beset by the same problems as amphibians. Those— mostly small—species which are exposed to regular enemies compensate with hypertrophical production of sex cells. Immense quantities of semen, eggs, and fingerlings are brought forth and devoured by fish and other predators. Fish that succeed in protecting their brood produce less. Often, among adult fish, finely balanced mutual-aid societies are established.

The ratios of eaters to their victims, and of violent to peaceful deaths, cannot be ascertained in the vast oceans. But ponds and aquariums can give us a pretty clear idea. Fish ponds in the Southeastern United States usually contain one predacious bass for every ten bluegills on which the bass feed. The bluegills and other forage fish, in turn, feed on bottom worms, insects, and vegetation. As far as the resulting weight is concerned, one bass weighs three times as much as the bluegill bream or sunfish that it eats.

The food chain starts out with green algae, which provide the pond with oxygen and serve as nourishment to tiny crustaceans and polliwogs. These are relished by minnows and other fish two to four inches long. If the green plants were not transformed into minnow-flesh, the larger game fish could not exist; and on the latter depends the well-being, if not the considerable bodyweight, of sportsfishermen. It is a very direct chain. 90 pounds of algae are needed for the upkeep of 30 pounds of minnows which, in turn, result in one pound of bass. When the bass dies in the pond without first being caught and pulled out by a fisherman, its mass is again transmuted into algae, worms, and tiny crustaceans. There is nothing terribly cruel about this recycling! Neither algae, minnows, nor bass are ever depleted; they reproduce their constant biomass, which means that most of them must die a natural death.

The Darwinian and Nietzschean dogma that warriors or predators are urgently needed to weed out the "unfit," the deformed, the sickly, and the weak individuals is a dubious idea. It cannot possibly hold true for the insects. For 200 million years the winged insects had the air all to themselves—there were no birds or bats around to exert selective pressure and improve the "lesser breeds." Nevertheless, as far as diversification, stamina, and morphological progress are concerned, the insects did very well indeed without being selectively eaten.

Since mesozoic times their breeding, feeding, and dying habits have changed fundamentally. Many modern insects have to be held in constant check by birds, bats, trout, wasps, and so on so that they won't become plagues.

This, however, is not the case with ants, which occur in larger quantities on earth than all other animals combined. Ants have spread over most of the earth's surface, and usually they fulfill tasks beneficial to their fellow creatures: cadaver disposal and prevention of contagious diseases, plowing and aerating the soil. Some ant species are overwhelmingly numerous; the colonies of *anomma,* for example, comprise up to 22 million. Yet their numbers do not normally need decimation through predation, they seem to remain high but constant. Only when species spread into new territories, (as does the fire-ant), do their populations explode to a dangerous degree.

The normal, specialized enemies of the ants happen to be quite ineffectual. The aardvark, the anteater *(myrmecophaga)*, echidna, dragonfly larvae, some spiders, and especially certain rapacious ants on the warpath do not manage to reduce the ants' number substantially. A horned toad has been observed to devour 65 desert ants in 30 minutes. Someone counted 1540 ants in 42 lizard stomachs. A European green woodpecker once swallowed 600 ants. Very impressive—but without any significance in reducing ant populations that are counted in millions or even billions.

Our panorama, though fragmentary, lends strong support to my overall estimate that only 5 percent of all animals are killed by other animals. (This figure disregards the creatures slaughtered by homo sapiens.) Ninety-five percent of all animal lives are terminated without bloodshed: by old age, sickness and exhaustion, hunger and thirst, changing climates, and the like. True, these kinds of death are often no less painful and gruesome than being torn to pieces or being swallowed alive. If they had the choice, many slowly starving creatures might prefer a speedy bite through the neck. Yet, since all living things have to die, we are not unjustified in preferring bloodless deaths. Seen philosophically, they throw a milder, friendlier light on our Mother Nature.

Ninety-five percent peaceful deaths—it certainly is a different picture from Tennyson's "nature, red in tooth and claw." But why do so many life-scientists still cling to a bloody and bloodthirsty interpretation of life? Sally Carrighar, in her beautiful book *Wild Heritage,* wrote that this impression "was derived chiefly from hunters, because, for a very long time, hunters were the only ones who penetrated the wildest areas. . . . Hunters, subconsciously or otherwise, tell about their experiences in terms as exciting and horrendous as possible."[5]

While there is a new breed of naturalists who shy away from macho generalizations, many neo-Darwinists still require the cruelties of natural selection as an integral part of their system. They continue to build on the cornerstone Darwin laid in 1859:

A struggle for existence inevitably follows from the high rate at which all organic beings tend to increase. Every being, which during its natural lifetime produces several eggs or seeds, must suffer destruction during some period of its life, and during some season or occasional year, otherwise, on the principle of geometrical increase, its numbers would quickly become so inordinately great that no country could support the product.[6]

If this were the general rule, we would not need to worry about the fate of the disappearing California condor, which usually lays only one egg every second year, or about bears giving birth to two cubs only once in two years. It seems fairly obvious that large creatures produce fewer descendants than small ones. It might even be a general rule that those animals which have few or no enemies tend to undergo few pregnancies. This natural birth control, which must be operative in many widely divergent species, is still very mysterious and urgently needs elucidation. Meanwhile, let us acknowledge—and possibly even enjoy the fact—that nature, left to her own devices, is more balanced and far less cruel than was dreamed of in neo-Darwinian philosophy.

Anyway, "weeding out the unfit" by force cannot be the decisive process that keeps our fauna healthy and progressing to ever higher efficiency levels. Hunting and trying to escape are very specialized activities; they cannot possibly be considered *the* sense of life. Encounters between the creatures of our planet rarely lead to combat; the social gamut runs from tolerance to outright helpfulness. Butterflies visit flowers not to harm them, but to enjoy each other.

Nevertheless, we read in modern biology books that "natural death is rather unnatural."[7] The most influential of all life scientists, Konrad Lorenz, says: "In nature, fighting is an ever-present process."[8] Many a sensitive youngster, when reading such generalizations, may ask: If nature is cruel, why should I be gentle and peaceful?

Darwin used his favorite terms "war of nature" and "struggle for survival" interchangeably. But is a plant that tries to survive at a desert's edge really waging war, as Darwin theorized? This

stretches the concept of bellicosity to an almost perverse carica-
ture.

True, 50 million oyster eggs laid by a single oyster result in only
one surviving adult oyster; but this must be the most extreme case
of brood reduction. On the other end of the scale stands the Aus-
tralian koala. It has no natural enemies at all, except for the dingo
(an imported dog gone wild); it mates only every second year and
then produces a single offspring. Modern man hunted it almost to
the brink of extinction; in 1924, nearly 2 million koala pelts were
exported from Australia. Today, it is completely protected. The
koala best exemplifies the rule: no natural enemies—few pregnancies—no overpopulation.

This (tentative) law is also confirmed by the numerous species
whose progeny is rarely reduced through predation by other animals: various kinds of whale and dolphin, otter and skunk, bear
and tiger, pangolin, hedgehog and porcupine, eagle and ostrich,
and some species of seals and monkeys.

Nevertheless, Darwin proclaimed: "Very frequently it is not the
obtaining of food, but the serving as prey to other animals, which
determines the average numbers of a species."

This is certainly a wild exaggeration.

How did this bellicose concept of nature arise? In ancient times,
combat among humans was thought to bring out manly virtues;
consequently, war as such was not condemned as basically evil.
Still, generally speaking, the creation was considered to be harmonious, with everything having a preordained place. This hierarchic worldview changed drastically in the middle of the nineteenth century. In 1850, Alfred Tennyson wrote regretfully about
"Man . . . who trusted God was love indeed / and love Creation's
final law / Though Nature, red in tooth and claw / With ravin,
shrieked against his creed . . ." And Darwin, in 1859, postulated
"the struggle for life" in the title of his epoch-making work. It
was then that natural scientists put red glasses on their noses. That
nature is really not blood-red, but green, the color of hope, simply

could no longer be perceived. The relentless competition of early capitalism, ruthless exploitation, and bloody colonialism were justified as adhering to natural law, furthering the survival of the fittest.

Love itself became denatured and perverted into the battle of the sexes. Nietzsche's charming advice—"You go to woman? Don't forget the whip"—seemed the perfect act of oral vengeance for the sexual frustrations of the Victorian age. The painter Edvard Munch, that neurotic genius, presented his most attractive women as vampires, sucking blood from the neck of subdued males.

The worst consequences of this "hard" *Weltanschauung* were the Fascist frenzies of the 1930s and 1940s. "War alone keys up all human energies to their maximum tension," proclaimed Mussolini, and Hitler chimed in: "The very first essential for success is a perpetually constant and regular employment of violence." The deeds of these "philosopher-kings" matched their words.

Charles Darwin was a mild, highly cultured gentleman. But he could not escape the lifestyle of his epoch, which put a premium on the most uninhibited forms of competition. His most decisive example for the "struggle for existence" was a little plot of soil measuring three by two feet, which he had dug up, turned over, and freed from all vegetation. He then counted all weed seedlings that germinated in the spring: out of 357 plumules, 295 were killed, mostly by slugs and insects. This experiment gave rise to his far-flung theories. He did not establish mortality rates among mature plants and animals—and these are, after all, decisive for life on this planet. Had Darwin grown up, not in England, but in the California redwoods, he might have counted perhaps three individual trees dying every year of old age in the thousand-year-old groves. The picture of nature interminably devouring itself might then never have occurred to him.

Biosophical observation gives us the right to call life a mostly peaceable endeavor. Naturally it is natural to die a natural death!

We know this. But do the generals and admirals know? How

absurd that the military establishments hold in readiness the equivalent of fifteen tons of dynamite for every man, woman, and child on this globe!

It's not only the primitive drives welling up from our ancestral "reptilian brain" deep inside our cerebrum. Often our so-called rational thinking produces ideologies which, for a few decades, seem so clear and justified that we are willing to eliminate all divergent ideas.

One person is sacrificed on an Aztec altar by having his living heart ripped out; another is burnt at the stake because he cannot believe that the dough of the Host is actually the body of Christ; someone has to mount the guillotine because liberty, equality, and fraternity are realized that way; someone else is rotting in an arctic labor camp because this furthers the classless society; yet another is sprayed with burning napalm to learn the blessings of democracy. For these individuals it can hardly be a consolation that only a tiny percentage of manking perishes this way. If only the human spirit could be widened to acknowledge that there is no such thing as justified cruelty!

For life's sake, we should be able to find out what life is all about! Is the process of living only the winding down of a chemo-electric clockwork? Has being alive an absolute value? Are the numerous suicides right to negate life as such? Or are the heart surgeons right to take infinite care to prolong life? Both cannot be right—not in relation to the subject of life itself.

Is the boundless grief of a loving mother seeing her child die a more correct attitude than the doing-a-job mentality of a bombardier pressing a lever to pulverize humans below?

Riddles, unanswerable riddles.

And yet, life is right here! We are not dealing with spiral nebulae in unattainable distances, nor with the earth's core hidden from our perception. You and I, we are brimful of life. We should be able to grasp it. Being constantly buffeted and blown about by the play and counterplay of living forces, we have an interior view of life; must we still ask in the end: What was it really, this life? It has flitted by, motley or grey, sometimes delightful, sometimes over-whelmingly gruesome. It was mine, but what was it?

Can a philosopher say much more than a bartender consoling his dejected customer: Such is life . . . ?

We have to accept life on its own terms. There are no others, at least none that apply to us. We have to talk about "good" or "bad" even while conscious of the obvious relativity of such valuations. "Good for whom?" we have to ask before every decision. The more general the applications of this "good," the more desirable. The mounting scale of positive values would appear, consequently, like this: good for my own self, for my family, for my club, my community, my ideological or religious group, for my province, nation, continent, for humanity, in ever widening circles. Only when we come to the most general aim—good for life—is relativity suspended, allowing us to envisage an obligatory good.

Similarly, we must use the terms "large" and "small" as if they offered a clearly defined meaning, even while knowing that they mean only large or small in relation to our median human stature of five-and-a-half feet. Therefore no value-judgment is implied: "small" never means inconsequential or inferior; the inner structure of a cell is as perfect as the whole organism to which it belongs.

Protagoras held that man was the measure of all things. A healthy pride went with that dictum and permeated much of the ancient world. Only when Copernicus and Newton overturned that world view did we acquire a collective inferiority complex. Bernard de Fontenelle, in 1686, told of a lady who, when she was informed of the new natural science, complained: "This universe is too big, I lose myself in it. I don't know any more where I am, I am nothing any more. Earth is so frighteningly small!"

Yet human beings cannot be disdained because the planet on which we live seems only a speck of dust compared to the Milky Way. We are as big as we are!

We hear it said: "Man looks up to the stars and nebulae and feels completely inconsequential." But this has no objective meaning; otherwise, we could turn the phrase around: "Man searches the atom for its tiniest particles and feels immensely significant." Why does nobody say that? Because man is his own measure. "Large" is an organism that is larger than the average vertebrate. The whale is gigantic, palpably so; exactly as a hummingbird is visibly tiny. And that's the long and the short of it. Man is just normal. We should not be too modest for the wrong reasons; we have enough other faults that could warrant some modesty.

Blaise Pascal recognized this in the seventeenth century: "What, lastly, does man amount to in nature? A nothing compared to infinity, a cosmos compared to nothingness, a middle between nothing and all."

Surprisingly, this intuitive localization was confirmed by Arthur Eddington in the twentieth century: "Approximately in the medium range between atom and star we find a no less admirable entity —the human body. About 10^{27} atoms make up this body; about 10^{28} human bodies would deliver enough matter to form an average star."

The figure ten, followed by 26 zeroes towards the interior—by 27 zeroes towards the exterior: this symmetry is quite amazing. To form the center: indeed a cosmic task for humans.

But let us not forget another localization for homo sapiens, this one applied by the sober Montaigne: "Elevated to the world's highest throne, we are still always sitting on our own behind."

All in all: life is a wonderful adventure!

Should we pronounce this sentence with a wormy conscience, considering wars and chicanery, deprivation and discouragement around us? Is love for life today something to be ashamed of? Can it only be generated by naive, old-fashioned optimism? I don't think so. I am convinced that this is the correct description of a fact: Life is a desirable good.

The main reason for this lies in the flexibility of the human psyche, which can find ways to escape from almost every kind of misery. We are not built to be unhappy twenty-four hours a day. We possess the faculty to generate feelings of happiness within ourselves. Strictly speaking, we do not really feel happiness; for the "happy feeling" is not an input of our sense organs, as are "green" and "warm." This means that the relation "always when, then" does not apply to the occurrence of happiness. Someone who perceives the taste of chocolate as happiness per se may then overeat and experience the same taste as repulsive. Not even the sex act affords us a guarantee for pleasure-gain. Happiness is created deep within ourselves.

Poets describe the feeling of the breast bursting with delight. Physiologically, this may be nonsense; but phenomenologically it is a valid description of the ego's transcendence of its normal bounds, which is characteristic during blissful times. Grief makes us contract, happiness expands us.

A person who has a happy temperament can feel contentment gazing at the evening star through the bars of a prison window. A person who is forced to attend an official banquet, eat caviar, and drink champagne may be bored and unhappy. A person with a sense of humor may see funny caricatures in the people around him, while a fourth may be frightened by these same visages. There is no standard to these experiences, the potential for happiness differs in each human being. But though everyone may have a different happiness, every human knows happiness.

In spite of the unbridgeable individuation, happiness seems to be very contagious. A happy being can—by dint of suggestion, explanation, example, or induction—produce the possibility of delight (or at least of joy) in a fellow being. As a boy I once left a neighbor's house with my mother; it had just rained, and puddles covered the street. "Nasty mud!" my mother complained. I contradicted: "Look at the pretty reflections of the clouds in the puddles!" Her face lit up, and she let me help her cross the little lakes. "This is exactly like jumping through the sky," she smiled.

Our capacity for happiness is an invaluable possession. We should cultivate it more consciously, not only for our own sake, but to make the earth a friendlier abode.

Of course nobody can tell with certainty what is going on inside another person's consciousness. However, there is always a strong tendency to draw analogies. Schiller even maintained: "Lust was given to the worm." How did he know, not having been a worm himself? Does a poet perhaps know the feelings of a worm better than the worm itself?

Braving the risk that I might only be projecting the contents of my psyche, I maintain: Every higher-organized animal experiences, for some moments at least, undiluted delight. I believe that every human soul is so independent from external conditions that at times it breaks out into irrational jubilation. The occasion may simply be the overflowing of an endocrine gland; that does not matter. How glorious it is sometimes to feel alive, to exist!

We may have become too cynical to acknowledge that the best things in life are free. Still: for some of our best experiences we don't have to pay, neither with money nor with a hangover.

Advancement, in a mechanistic, one-dimensional sense, is not an adequate mold into which our existence should be poured. Theoretically, we could imagine a child recognizing a well-defined purpose and hurrying unfailingly toward the attainment of this aim. In practice, this is never the case. Considering the multiplicity of our possibilities, the "straight and narrow path" isn't even desirable.

Efficient, linear advancement: We find it in the progress of a pig from its mother's tits to the bacon factory.

Compared to that, it is even preferable that we occasionally feel our lives to be senseless. But we must not yield to the nefarious temptation of objectivizing this subjective feeling. Like the *taedium vitae* of the declining Roman empire, we must consider the contemporary existential *nausée* as a temporary phenomenon caused and also overcome by the *zeitgeist*. Some people feel this senselessness regularly each afternoon before cocktail hour. Some are apt to feel it most strongly during menopause. Disgust with life is always bound up with time; as time passes, so the tedium evaporates. Of course it is hard to keep this in mind during the hours of nausea and surfeit.

No human life forms the shortest, straightest line between the two points of birth and death. No river presents itself on a map as a straight line; and yet, considering all the interfering forces and influences, it forms the most economical downward course. How willful and capricious the loops and detours of a stream appear, seen from an airplane! But as soon as we put the dimensions of elevation and time into the descriptive formula, the apparent unruliness disappears. Perhaps, in depreciating an individual life or a historical period, we just don't see the depth-dimension that would make it intelligible.

To some of us life appears "deep"—that is, transparent enough to let some significance shine through. It seems full of exciting problems, mysterious moods, multiple dimensions, some undefineable sense that is more important than smooth functioning. In this view a string quartet by Beethoven, a poem by Shelley or Hölderlin discloses more of the spirit's role in the world than all our statistics and analyses.

But, strangely enough, this depth-dimension cannot be demonstrated. It is impossible to explain the immense significance of existence to a philistine, he simply will not recognize what we call depth. Does this cancel out this depth-dimension? Is life "really" flat and insignificant?

No, this the philistine cannot prove to me—just as I cannot show the deep significance of the human experience to him.

The great ideas of humanity do not suffice to fill a human life. You cannot meditate twenty-four hours a day; you cannot always reside in the thin air of pure reason. The anima which, to other times and cultures, seemed eternal and indestructible, is superseded and even replaced in the course of every day by the prosaic mechanics of staying alive. The bodily needs push cognition aside.

The compensation for this insufficiency lies in the knowledge that even the most sublime ideas are intimately connected to physiological grounds. Death! What a huge, horrifying concept! And yet the fear of death was simply a biological necessity to counteract the destruction of a species: only those individuals who were able to evade dangers would thrive and multiply. And the enormously impressive, evident horror of death is only a trick of nature, it is not a given fact of the physical cosmos. Without the subjectively repulsive, terror-producing component of lethal experience, the process of dying would not provoke such a negative value judgment.

And the same applies to love. How exalted, noble, beautiful, fulfilling is the love experience! But what is behind it? The biologically founded, innate, and selectively reinforced drive to eliminate or at least to postpone extinction. Whoever among living beings would not be endowed with the wish and with the mechanism for propagation would die out in the first generation. A mutation that deprived a race of the capacity for love would be doomed.

Does this mean that the fear of death, the bliss of love, are errors, illusions of our interior view of life?

Yes and no. Here a phenomenon that Schopenhauer called "the ruse of reason" becomes effective. In one view, admittedly, we are lumps of flesh. For us, nothing is more satisfying, more correct than to follow those few basic drives toward permanence and progress. This is what justifies our existence: our harmonious accord with the immanent mission of life over millions of years. The unorganized droplet of protoplasm and the lyric poet follow the same instinct.

Value is that which a *subject* esteems *objectively;* an antinomy that cannot be resolved within the verbal sphere.

Beauty is "only" a function of life; therefore it cannot be absolute. Wherever colors, shapes, sounds, and smells serve to attract another living being, we have to surmise the impression of beauty. This may be a circular definition, but we are dealing here with the rounding of the life cycle. The relativity of beauty concepts does not make them useless; on the contrary, it integrates them into relationships, it anchors them firmly in life.

By now we should be accustomed to the switched roles of the antithetical concepts of "absolute" and "relative." Their modern meaning really corresponds more exactly to their literal origin. "Relative" means in connection to, or founded in the web of phenomena. "Absolute" means loosened from, ergo: unfounded.

This is just the opposite of the naive usage. We can no longer escape from acknowledging relativity in all possible fields and utilizing it for new insights.

The relativists have been victorious in the most varied branches of science. Physics of the smallest and largest ranges cannot do without Einstein's theories. Aesthetics and theology have had to give up one absolute dogma after the other. Ethics, once a closed system of generally applicable precepts that were thought to be demonstrable in a geometric manner, is split up and relativized: exotic and primitive behavior modes can hardly be brought into harmony with occidental customs. Relativity had its triumphal procession through all fields of human endeavor.

But now, after this victory, the relativists should permit themselves to become more human again.

Humaneness, dignity, love of neighbor, quality of life: all these are not exactly defineable concepts; and yet they should revert to their regulatory capacity. "Life for life's sake": this sentence could become the constant around which a new system of coordinates and references may be erected. There are still so many variables that we can ill afford not to use this regulative. Life, in its concreteness and multiformity, with its stupid and wise volitions, with its egotistical needs and altruistic will to sacrifice: This must be our Archimedean point of leverage. Without this reference we will hardly be able to conquer the problems of the near future.

Life for life's sake. This axiom comprises Albert Schweitzer's "veneration for life" as well as Goethe's insight, "Life produces all living things."

Life relates to itself and, therefore, provides its own quasi-absolute valuation. Everything that furthers life is, by itself, good—because the concept "good" exists only for living beings. This leads on to such regulating principles as peacefulness, tempered justice, humane administration, benevolence in its broadest application.

This must be the direction of our biosophical explorations—for life's sake.

2. The Sense of Biological Development

"A prejudiced judge!" cried the stinkweed when I pulled it out, leaving the parsley beside it alone.

Is there an immanent direction to life as we know it on earth?

Looking back over the millions of years during which life left traces behind, we can observe four tendencies that seem to inhabit organic matter.

First: Life wants to preserve itself.

Second: Life wants to spread.

Third: Life wants to satisfy itself.

Fourth: Life wants to refine itself.

Concerning the first point: *Life has an inherent tendency to preserve itself,* living matter wants to stay alive. The drive to self-preservation is an extraordinary phenomenon, compared to the inanimate cosmos. True, suns and planets hold themselves together through gravitation, counteracting centrifugal forces that strive to disperse them. Likewise, a drop of water falling from the faucet through the air does not let go of its particles; its cohesion saves its molecules from bursting out of the drop's shape. But as soon as it has fallen into the basin, it spreads irrevocably. The same molecules will never again combine to form the identical drop, the drop as entity has ceased to exist. Life is basically different. The same biochemical combination that formed a few molecules a billion years ago still exists in you—life has never been exterminated and re-created. At least one particle or principle inside you is indeed a billion years old! It can make you dizzy trying to gaze thus into the depth of time. The fragile, soft, exposed protoplasm, activated from within, is more stable than the passive, weather-beaten rock or the hardest iron, which is soon eaten away by rust.

In order to protect itself against the icy and fiery menaces of the cosmos and against the utter indifference, inertia, and catastrophic instability of its earthly surroundings, life was able to rely on two protective, motoric forces: hunger and love. Hunger forced each living unit to replace its used-up matter by ingesting fresh material, thus guaranteeing enough storage of new fuel. Hunger, already given to the earliest unicellular being, watched over the preservation of the individual; and love tended to the preservation of the species. Even while life complicated itself to an incredible degree, these most primitive vectors inside almost all living matter remain irresistible.

Concerning our second point: *Life strives to spread its domain.* Never and nowhere does it shrink voluntarily into a smaller area. It never relinquishes its once-established reign, it always tries to convert more and more anorganic matter into organic stuff. As higher organisms, we ourselves depend entirely on this rapaciousness: We feed on organic matter that has already been digested— the oftener the better. (The obvious exceptions to this rule are salts, water, and trace elements: these materials we ingest directly from the inanimate crust of the earth.) Thanks to the expansion principle, the biosphere comprises almost the entire temperate surface of this planet; and we conquer arctic wastes, deep mines, and the moon for the domain of life.

The third tendency that inhabits living matter is *the drive to satisfaction*. We can almost call it life's self-indulgence. The other three tendencies are subordinated to this one: self-preservation, spreading, and refining serve to improve the conditions that warrant the gratification of life's drives and whims.

Our vital, primary drives such as hunger, thirst, sexual lust, the need to breathe, to sleep, to defecate, and so on are endowed with a tremendous urgency, they demand irresistibly that life should serve them—to the extent that even the menace of death cannot deter a being from satisfying these needs.

However, we cannot count among these primary drives those which are not essential for life's continued existence. The will to power, the ownership and defense of a strictly circumscribed territory, sadistic and masochistic lusts are not irresistible. As Konrad Lorenz has shown, the drive to aggression can be sidetracked, replaced by rituals, and rendered innocuous. A creature that submits to the power drive of another, or that must evade the territorial expansion of a neighbor can still live. Frustrations like these are not deadly. Harm to our cultural patterns is bearable until reform or revolution makes our circumstances viable again, or until we resign ourselves once and for all. But hunger and thirst know no resignation, they demand to be satisfied under penalty of death. Unfulfilled sexual longing often makes life appear devoid of any sense—which, though not lethal, is sometimes worse than death. In the psychic realm the need for love is as urgent as the more direct drives to physical incorporation. From here life's drive toward satisfaction leads on toward the highest spheres of spiritualization.

This connects to our fourth proposition: *Life wants to refine itself.* This tendency may be the least self-evident, yet it is just as important to the fourfold path of life.

What is meant here by refinement? It is the difference between the salamander groping through mud, thick, vulnerable, and clumsy, and the slender, firm, agile, and graceful lizard; between the scaly, unadorned, flowerless liverwort and the showy, highly differentiated orchid; between the swarthy, phlegmatic tapir and the nervous, spirited horse; between the physically overpowering, shaggy gorilla and the highly trained, elegant airplane pilot. Refinement amounts to complication, specialization, intellectualization, progress. All this is part of the concept of refinement: an entire range of independent but parallel modifications of a creature's *gestalt* and behavior.

The same basic drive to complexity which turns a fat, featureless larva into a shimmering, mobile butterfly is still active in our own cultural endeavors. Through this identical drive, we have transmuted oxcarts into space shuttles and clay tablets into electronic word processors. I sense it even in music's development from simple Gregorian plainsong to Bach's miraculously intricate

"Art of the Fugue" and to the overpowering orchestrations of Bartók and Stravinsky.

Simply as description of a known phenomenon, the mounting refinement in the phylogenesis of most organisms cannot be denied. Is it immanent in life as such? Progressive complications, specialized organization, ever-more attractive embellishments are so clearly observable that it is easy to take them as part of the process of living.

You don't have to believe in mystical forces to register this general improvement of the biosphere.

Everyone who strives for a wide-angle view of life must acknowledge that the human being is actually the avant-garde of a one-way development which we can designate as progress or, leaving aside all value judgments, as complication. This racial improvement in time is quite comparable to the growing-up of an individual. Why do single organisms grow? The growth faculty in one living being is not dependent on Darwinian selection, it is pre-formed in the living matter: for the cell-splitting multiplication, the progressive conglomeration of more and more cells are not necessarily more advantageous in the struggle for existence than the stubborn conservatism of one solitary, dim-witted cell floating around.

In the same way, the morphological variegation, the directed complication and augmented refinement of certain favored or adventurous races are not the result of natural selection; they are autonomous functions of living matter.

In life's realm growth is an all-pervasive principle. No tree shrinks in old age to become a seed, it only becomes rotten and fragmented and finally collapses. No living thing remains stationary. Growth is a basic tendency of all organizable matter.

But certain inhibitions curtail the unlimited growth of any organism. Interchange is needed to maintain the activity of any life system, the slags must be eliminated, nourishment has to be ingested and distributed to all organs for refueling the metabolism. Any crude increase in massiveness to further and maintain these mechanisms is impractical, because the surface of a growing ball is augmented proportionally much slower than its content, and only the surface can manage the needed interchange with the surroundings. The membrane that encloses the cell and permits the desired juices to filter through becomes the more inadequate the larger the cell grows. This purely geometric insufficiency of the spherical cellular surface is the reason why cells must partition and multiply: they have the inner need to provide more surfaces for the bartering processes of the organism.

Yet even the partitioning principle does not suffice to fulfill the mounting need for circulation. Therefore those creatures who somehow were impregnated with the will to grow will develop ever more differentiated and variegated organs—still just following their initial tendency toward growth. Soon grotesque protuberances, leaves and pseudo-fins, tentacles and warts and nipples augment the surface through which the nourishing surroundings can be utilized by a creature. A loosely knit sponge, raggedy and shot through with holes, is the extreme result of this drive.

The insects never quite realized the advantages of optimal circulation and, consequently, could never grow as big as some vertebrates. When they developed their—structurally needed—skeletons on the outside and refined them into armor, they cut off the interchange with their environment. Spiders, lice, butterflies receive their oxygen through complicated tubes connected directly to the air. Since no inner circulation transports the oxygen throughout the body, land insects of human size would suffocate. The largest dragonfly of all time only reached a wing-span of 70 centimeters. Nonetheless, this branch of life, the arthropods, pushed their differentiation very far; what seems lacking in them is dynamism, individual initiative, the joy of experimenting with ever-new biological forms; this remained to the vertebrates. Thus the warm-blooded land-dweller have won the race of progress—a literally "breath-taking" race.

Any species that would have this tendency toward growth and enhanced activism—in its individuals or as an inheritable drive—must have found it necessary to strive for higher degrees of complication. Intensified metabolism was advantageous and could only be managed through increasingly complicated physiological mechanisms. Do we need more explanations for the amazing phylogenetic progress of life? As soon as the principle of variegation was imprinted on life as a useful tendency, the development toward higher and higher refinement knew no bounds.

Thus assiduity and acquisitiveness became closely connected; and acquisitiveness had to work through the sensations of hunger, thirst, sex drive, and the need to breathe. Ordinarily, our periodic craving for fresh air is hardly noticed; but it is as irresistible and important as the other drives. It made all the difference between the degree of progressiveness in insects and in vertebrates. This is the reason why our industrial air pollution is so dangerous: Its depressing effect makes our lives something less than human.

Perhaps in the future we will dine on petroleum steaks and algae pies that won't cost a penny. When this happens, the economic difference between air, water, and food will have disappeared—victuals, drinks, and air for breathing will be equally accessible to everyone. Will this put an end to the assiduity we inherited from our vertebrate forebears? On the contrary. The drive to vital activity and refinement, liberated from the slavery of making money, will progress into freely selected endeavors. The need to be active and ever more multifarious has been implanted into human nature by nature herself.

But these speculations are premature.

The innate drive toward refinement and complication finds its expression in many biological phenomena. The sometimes fantastic length and intricacy of the intestines are essential for the interchange between an organism and its surroundings; they are quite surprising compared to the relatively small outer surface of the belly in which they are enclosed. The same holds true for the highly developed brain with the multiple folds of gray rind in which the thought processes take place. Certainly this complication corresponded to the normal tendency of organic matter through many previous stages. Seeds, eggs, and larvae are always less variegated than the mature end results.

Admittedly, the selection of the fittest to survive the struggle for existence is a powerful source for this enhanced complication; but does it fully explain the general tendency? Intelligence—the result of the rising complication of the primates' brains—is really not that advantageous, compared to such life-saving devices as thick, hairy skin, increased fertility, speed, prominent claws, and teeth. These could be just as useful to a developing race as intelligent behavior. The plain fact that the stupid beings continue to exist side by side with the smarter ones would seem to demonstrate their fitness for life on this earth.

Does this not make it probable that the road to higher intelligence is an innate tendency (at least of apes and hominids) independent of natural selection through elimination of the duller individuals?

Teilhard de Chardin called human beings "the ascending arrow in the great biological synthesis."[9] This is well put, considering the incredibly augmented reach and refinement of human perception. Our senses have been extended to the spiral nebulae, our maximum speed has reached cosmic figures. As far as complication and extension of our influence are concerned we should be proud indeed. At the least this immense potential entails obligations of the highest order.

The innate will to refinement and complication seen in the development of most living forms should eventually be demonstrable in the sex cells of organisms, just as biochemists are already able to trace and understand growth hormones and molecular mechanisms of heredity. Science will doubtless find out why single-celled creatures grow, divide, and multiply, but why don't these split cells stay together to build up larger organisms? Meanwhile, it is still an enigma why unicellular beings continue to live exactly as they did at the beginning of life on the planet, while other cells have the inherent wish to become multicellular beings.

On every stage of life's development conservative species refuse to take part in the general movement toward innovation and sophistication. Archaic forms such the amoeba, the horseshoe crab

(Xiphosurus), the shark, and many others have, through unthinkably long periods, continued to procreate identical individuals without ever changing their shapes or functions. It is misleading to call them living fossils, because they are as vital as any modern species. According to strictly mechanical evolutionary theories these primitive creatures should have been displaced and superseded by better-equipped animals. Instead we find that the opossum, the only surviving American marsupial, keeps spreading: Formerly at home only in the Middle Atlantic states of North America, it was later observed in New England, and nowadays it multiplies freely in California. Why this unintelligent little beast has left its special niche, and why it is so successful, nobody seems able to explain.

Biologists may prove with statistics and computers that the blind chance of purposeless mutations adds up to the refinement and progress of so many otherwise divergent species. Perhaps they will some day find a complication-hormone or a molecular mechanism that causes ever-growing sophistication. We'll have to await clarification. I admit that I'm inclined toward the second alternative, or to even more dynamic explanations; an immanent drive toward the refinement of life holds for me a biosophical fascination. I know that this is not an empirical, scientific point of view. But as a working hypothesis, the innate one-way directedness of life must still be strongly considered.

The four congenital tendencies of life—self-preservation, expansion, the need for satisfaction, and progressive refinement—will appear even more fundamental if we turn our question around: What does life *not* want?

Life does not want to be painless. Even though each individual being hates the sensation of pain and tries to avoid it, this does not influence the will and development of its species. Natural selection works against such an accommodation. An animal that eliminated the warning pressure of pain in its nervous system would son fall prey to dangers and wounds and would thus leave no pain-free offspring. Life accepts the appropriate occurrence of hurt and suffering.

Further: *Life does not want 100 percent safety*. In Central European forests one can hear the mountain-cock emitting his gurgling love-cry to impress his hen. When he opens his beak, his ear canal is pinched shut, and he is thus physically incapable of diverting his attention from his ardent wooing. The hunter knows this, approaches, and ends the love song with a bullet. This seems a rather purposeless arrangement; and, according to Darwin's theory, the mountain-cock should be extinct. He is now protected not by Darwinian but by human law.

The impetus of just being alive sometimes intoxicates animals to a degree that they disregard their safety. This enthusiasm has no place in the theoretical system of "survival of the fittest." A peacock wants to display his varicolored plumage even if this converts him into a provocative target. A songbird wants to produce his full-throated song without considering it an advertisement to preying meat-eaters. The need for safety is not always and not everywhere the supreme law. Abandon to the pure joy of existence cannot be suppressed all the time. Life wants to feel adventurous—on occasion.

Another, rather surprising, paradox is this: *Life does not want longevity*. Even though each individual wishes to postpone its own death as long as possible, this longing has no effect on the evolutionary development of the various species. No warm-blooded animal lives as long as the—much more primitive—turtle *Testudo sumeiri*, which has been observed to live for as long as 152 years. The maximum natural lifespan of a healthy, well-fed Neanderthal man was possibly not shorter than the maximum allotted time of a modern man. The strivings of each individual don't add up to an inheritable result, even though they point in the same direction for many millennia.

The explanation for this regrettable state of affairs lies, for a change, in natural selection. Growing very old individually is no advantage for a race, for its procreation, conservation, and spread. The selection for longevity would be without inheritable effect because most animals reproduce during the first third of their existence. The oldsters that remain on the earth after most of their generation has died off may be "the fittest" as far as endurance is concerned; but they have died a "genetic death" long before their individual demise, their sperm glands and ovaries have become ineffectual—their qualities will not be part of the profile of the following generations. The senile wish to linger on for a while cannot be brought to fruition in the next generation, it dies out with each specimen.

However, other tendencies of living matter are definitely inheritable and add up, through generations, to a clear trend. Perhaps the most important current is the following: *Life tends to become more beautiful.* The drab, flowerless horsetails that prevailed during the Carbon age were less pretty than modern daisies and orchids. A primitive worm is uglier than a highly differentiated, shimmering butterfly or beetle. An archaic shark or ray is esthetically inferior to our modern rainbow trout or to the jewel-like fish of the coral reefs. The uncouth Coelacanth looks deplorable compared to its descendants, the motley salamanders and glittering lizards. Saltoposuchus, the half-reptilian ancestor of birds, was not as lovely as our finches and parakeets. And, finally, a gorilla is just not as beautiful as homo sapiens.

These developments are by no means all-pervasive. There are many modern animals and plants which, for us, have not the slightest aesthetic value. Yet there are also ravishingly beautiful beings—and these are, to an overwhelming degree, products of our own Cenozoic age. Embellishment, as a component of the general tendency toward refinement, is of utmost importance: it has transformed our environment.

Of course we must keep in mind what the pre-Socratic philosopher Epicharmos said: "For the donkey, the donkey mare is the most beautiful." A considerable subjectivity in aesthetic judgments belongs to the variegation of life. But this does not prevent aesthetic judgments from converging toward congruity whenever various subjects agree in many habits, functions, and preferences.

The very obvious tendency toward aesthetic enhancement remains unmentioned in run-of-the-mill biology books. Still, even mechanistically oriented life scientists admit some special series of purposeless embellishment. They acknowledge, almost in bad humor, that the Argus pheasant, the peacock, the bird of paradise disregarded the advantages of free mobility and camouflage in favor of impressing their females. A hen or doe, having to choose between several males, selected that husband who had longer or more colorful appendages—feathers or antlers—than his rivals. This repeatedly preferred peculiarity then became an inherited trait of the offspring.

Darwin, who cannot be suspected of sentimental aestheticism, even opined that men developed their beautiful beards in order to please the choosy ladies. He doubted, however, whether high intellectual faculties were caused by this selection, because male intelligence has no sex-appeal for women.

"Sexual selection," as Darwin called this principle, was in his view almost as decisive for evolution as "natural selection," the survival of the fittest. Recent biologists disregard this vector toward beautification, simply because beauty cannot be formulated in numbers and graphs. Sexual selection is not even mentioned in some self-styled "Darwinist" textbooks. And yet it is a decisive factor in the formation of higher forms of life.

The title of Darwin's epoch-making work is usually abbreviated *The Origin of Species.* The unshortened title is more explicit: *On the Origin of Species by Means of Natural Selection, or the Preservation of Favoured Races in the Struggle for Life.*

Darwin was willing to consider the well-formed and beautifully colored as "favoured races." Most of his followers admitted armor, speed, and drab mimicry as the only signs of fitness. From his long-winded title and many-faceted theme, only the "struggle for life" interested them.

A number of excellent geneticists see clearly that the elusive, subjective quality we call beauty poses a dilemma for the objective scientist. The following description by Theodosius Dobzhansky shows this difficulty.

As nearly as we are able to make it out, the biological function of all this glory of form and color is pragmatic: in animals it serves as species recognition marks in sexual unions. The real and unsolved problem is why these displays seem so superb also to man. There is no reason to think that females and males of the butterflies Ornithoptera or Morpho enjoy the sight of each other any more than do female and male lice and other creatures that we find repulsive.

Yet, in some situations it becomes really difficult not to impute to animals some sort of aesthetics. The performances of the bower birds, family Ptilorhynchidae, of which about nineteen species occur in Australia or New Guinea, are most extraordinary. At the approach of the mating season, the males build display grounds consisting of variously constructed "bowers" and "maypoles," to which they eventually entice females, and in or near which the matings take place. Nests, however, are built elsewhere. Most astonishingly, the bowers are decorated in various and often highly elaborate fashions. Some species cover an "avenue" approaching the bower with objects such as bleached animal bones, pieces of stone and metal, and silver coins if they can get them. Other species make a "meadow of moss," on which they arrange brightly colored fruits or flowers, which are there for display and are not eaten. Still others paint the walls of the bower with fruit pulp, or charcoal, or dry grass mixed with saliva. . . . Although his actions seem to be instinctive and automatic, it is impossible to deny that a well-adorned bower may give the bird a pleasure which can only be called aesthetic.[10]

The display of beauty must be more than just a signal to indicate to animals that they belong to the same species and can therefore proceed to sexual partnership; excessive ugliness would do the same. The drive toward beauty has a deeper sense; beauty is more than a sex-symbol, more than a green traffic light opening the way to copulation. Some natural scientists briefly mention the genetic importance of individual choice among potential sex partners for the development of new life-forms. Isaac Asimov acknowledges "the formation of species, whether through natural selection or through its variant, sexual selection."[11] But how can it be called a variant? The one selective process operates through love, the other through rapaciousness and death. Often they produce trends in opposite directions. They differ in the material on which they operate, in the forces that make them effective, in the aims and results of their selectiveness.

Sexual selection, as Darwin envisaged it, has been slighted by modern researchers in favor of the elaborate treatment accorded to the selection of the fittest through elimination of the unfit. By default, love as an evolutionary force has been left for biosophy to elucidate.

I would like to trace sexual selection beyond Darwin. I believe, for example, that the development from the little four-toed *Eohippus,* the extinct "dawn horse," to the one-hoofed, fast, high-strung *Equus caballus* was largely determined by the mares' preference for speedy stallions, and vice versa. Taste was the driving phylogenetic force. Orthodox genetics denies that something like the will of the species could ever have influenced any genealogical trend. One well-known biologist even complains about the popular illustrations in zoology books that show the step-by-step development from eohippus to the most recent model in a seemingly purposeful sequence. Beginning on the left, this popular series of pictures presents the precursor, about the size of a terrier, with rather short legs and three or four toes on each foot. In the intermediate stages the outer toes slide upward, no longer touch the soil, and eventually atrophy. (All these stages exist in fossil bones.) On the far right our *Equus* appears, large and proud, the end result of a directed, single-minded development. Nevertheless, we are supposed to believe that this one-way street was built accidentally, as though a highway could be constructed by throwing stones at random.

It has been proven that tiny variations in the genetic code of the DNA molecules are inheritable; but why should they add up to a certain trend? Variations—some for better, some for worse—would neutralize each other. The especially "horsy" mutations would not give decisive advantages over the earlier forms. Small five- and four-toed animals still populate the land today and prove merrily that they are fit for life.

If you have ever observed young mares and stallions gracefully playing in a pasture and feeling the awakening of love, you know that the young ladies show a special inclination toward fast, energetic equine gentlemen. This preference must have had cumulative results through the ages.

Even Franz Hančar, an excellent, pragmatically schooled connoisseur of horse lore and science, feels obliged to make his bow before orthodox genetics. He describes "the specialized development toward the runner of the Ice Age's steppes which has been gifted with speedy locomotion not only for the flight from dangers in the treeless environment, but also to reach its food with fleet feet."[12]

Are these arguments realistic? Grass never runs away; reaching a vegetarian feeding ground does not require speed. The dangers on the steppe were negligible, especially in North America. The wolf, probably the only important enemy of the horse, ate sick, old, and very young specimens. He always remained on the periphery of the herd, which means that the herd was better off staying together rather than dispersing willfully. The faster individuals are of no genetic advantage to the bulk of the herd. A mother mare who wants to protect her tiny foal has no need for speed: she does not want to run away from her offspring. Celerity in the steppe offers no advantages that would warrant the extinction of the slower forms.

Horses like to run fast; that is their psychological and physiological makeup. Grazing alone does not satisfy their craving for muscular activity. When domestic horses are allowed to join wild mustangs they change their personalities: They flourish in liberty, which, for a horse, means the liberty to run around. The joy of a horse able to race somewhat faster than its peers colors its entire habitus and makes it more active, proud, and eager to procreate. A horse that has been outrun several times by its competitors can develop an inferiority complex—it becomes odd, unable to work up the surplus of vital energy needed for erotic conquests. More or less complex reasons like these cause the speedier and more vital animals to prevail in nature's "war of succession." It is not at all necessary to assume that the less mobile ones are subjected to greater dangers and are physically eliminated by "the fittest."

We cannot study the behavior patterns of *Eohippus* and other extinct rungs on the evolutionary ladder; their bones don't betray love or hate. However, we know the habits of our *Equus caballus*. A stallion likes to assemble a harem of mares. To keep this harem under control, speed is indeed advantageous. A slow male horse would have a hard time watching over several females, circling around them, and keeping the eager young suitors at a respectful distance. If this harem psychology was already in effect with the early prefigurations of our horse, we would have an explanation for the enhancement of speed (at the expense of other qualities) that led to our one-toed contemporary. This would fall into the mold of Darwinian selection of the fittest: The fastest male becomes the owner of the largest harem and begets the greatest number of descendents.

Still, this would not be a victory for the combat mentality, but for the most efficient love-making. In many species, especially among the higher-organized ones, mutual admiration of males and females raises the level of beauty and efficiency and propels the race toward new, more refined, more perfect models.

Love, not war, is responsible for most of the progress of living creatures. This is an essential difference which, if confirmed by future biosophists, would brighten our entire outlook on life.

How effective is the "hard" principle of selection through suppressing and discarding the weaker forms of life? A toad fills its stomach with insects four times each summer day; it is estimated to eat 10,000 insects during each warm season. But does this decimation produce any noticeable improvement in the living apparatus of the surviving insects? No; the mosquito has remained the same through the eons.

On the other hand, such giant vegetarians as the elephant, rhino, and hippopotamus can never be eaten, and they never fight in competition for their food. Thus these enormous species were never subjected to competitive selection pressure toward higher fitness. Yet they kept healthy enough (that is, until man came along).

The Darwinian dogma required relentless combat: Without forceful elimination of the slower, smaller, stupider, and weaker mutations, every race was supposed to inherit these unfavorable traits and, consequently, to degenerate. This kind of eugenics relied, in the last analysis, on killing.

Against this theory we can maintain that felicitous mutations are more eager, willing, and able to procreate than their less-favored siblings. Sickly and misshapen specimens are kept occupied and distracted by their own bodily shortcomings; they cannot muster the surplus vitality needed for courtship or competitive wooing, for manufacturing seeds or pollen, ova or sperm, for the strenuous erotic rituals. They won't even enter into the arena, and thus they don't have to be shoved aside or killed by jealous rivals or by unwilling prospective mates. This takes care of congenital cripples and runts. Among the healthy and fertile male animals, the successful males will either please the females or drive competitors away. Various animals have a wide array of psychological motives that can influence their procreative decisions: admiration and envy, sense of beauty, trust or distrust, authority, jealousy, frigidity, or insatiable sex appetite. All these are by no means confined to the human psyche, they are part of the individual motivation of the more developed animals, and they will modify the blind chance of genetic variations.

Psychotherapists have shown that an inferiority complex often leads to impotency. Why should this connection be confined to the human species?

Konrad Lorenz uses bison, antelopes, and horses to demonstrate that the attitude of combat between rivals inside a certain species "leads to the evolution of particularly strong and courageous defenders of family and herd. . . . This interaction has produced impressive fighters such as bull bison or the males of the large baboon species."[13] Fight and competition always! Lorenz never supposes that healthy and useful racial developments—like that from *Eohippus* to *Equus*—might be caused by friendly selection among the breeding partners. For him, erotic preferences can only lead to "colorful feathers, bizarre forms" and similar "nonsense"!

Sexual selection, according to Lorenz, drives a species "into the most stupid blind alley of evolution."[14]

Many exact scientists want to avoid anthropomorphic views: For too long people have considered inanimate things such as winds, planets, rivers as male and female entities. Not only poets spoke of "my brother Sun, my sister Moon." Consequently, nowadays science bends over backwards to deny that animals can possess volition, taste, and initiative.

Yet such widely differing creatures as shimmering butterflies, long-feathered peacocks, and speedy horses have surely developed their distinctive exaggerations through long and repetitive preference as to their mates. It was not the dying-out of the lesser-equipped individuals that determined many higher racial forms, but the choice of partners according to erotic and aesthetic points of view. *Life itself wants to become more full-blooded, stronger, shinier —more glorious.*

In my view, it is entirely plausible that the selective breeding from Neanderthal man to homo sapiens was caused by erotic and aesthetic preferences between sexual partners. Millions of acts of free choice added up to the most brilliant development in the entire realm of life. Through the ages choosy youths and finicky virgins favored partners with a high forehead, upright bearing, straight, long limbs, smoother and less hairy skin. All these single steps in the same direction have accomplished a fantastically significant journey.

At this point we need to define a biosophical concept that differs from all acknowledged principles of today's schoolbook biology— namely, *aesthetic selection.*

The process of aesthetic choice by selective mates (and, to a lesser degree, by members of a herd or a symbiotic group) is responsible for a great number of phenomena. Selection through taste preferences produced impractical luxury forms, such as showy plumage, exuberant fins, ornamental horns, baroque cock's combs. Aesthetic selection also produced the eminently practical enhancement of increasingly attractive fruits and blossoms. This selective principle works through sensibilities of the eye, the palate, the sex appetite; it functions by dint of—primitive but undeniable—value judgments. We may state that sensuality serves progress: a thought that would have been abhorrent to the Victorian mentality.

Sensual acts of preference discard dull, drab, colorless, uninteresting individuals. Aggressive selection, on the other hand, eliminates weakness and sickness, lack of skill or speed, foolhardiness, conspicuousness of color and form, cowardice, and fatalism. Although it tends to rid life of many faults and frailties, it also disposes of much individual fancy and whimsy. The mechanism of violent "Darwinian" selection uses killing, starving, hurting, fatigue, chasing from nest and home, brood destruction; in short, it uses those innumerable "evil" deeds with which one creature can harm another.

Sexual and aesthetic selections, on the contrary, work through "good" actions, at least from our point of view. They produce light signals (as in glowworms and deep-sea fish), colorful display, dancing, wooing rites, lovely song, gift offerings to the chosen one, enticing shapes and smells, personal grooming, and gentleness in order to appear attractive.

Purely aesthetic selection (without sexual purpose) causes berries on our bushes to turn showy red, thus attracting birds that will eat these fruits and distribute the pits far and wide in their excrements for new germination. The same aesthetic selection (sometimes with sexual overtones) manages the development of fragrances in nature: Flowers and animals learn to boardcast smell signals. The musk rose and the musk deer produce chemically different but equally seductive smells that attract bees, musk doe, and gentlemen who appreciate musky perfume on highly civilized ladies. It is not necessary for cherries and apples to taste good in order to be fertile; the connection between these two qualities is developed for the benefit of fruit-eaters.

In the realm of blooming plants the victorious competitor is not that flower which manufactures and distributes its pollen in the most practical way, but the one which packages it most attractively. Considering a flower solely as a mechanism of fertility, the most streamlined transport of male pollen to a female pistil would entirely suffice. The complicated appendages for offering honey, for emitting fragrances and colored light rays have nothing to do with the procreative function as such. Nectar serves as a reward for the "right" behavior of the fertilizing insect. The recompense is twofold: the blossom that first happened to produce some slightly sweetish liquid trained the primitive precursors of our bees to learn its markings and to find them again and again. This fed the "learned" insects better than the stupid ones, thus causing them to multiply. Through this numerical advantage the signals of the favored blossoms were augmented, so that the mutual benefits served to enhance the aesthetic makeup through many millennia.

Some early pomes, by accidental mutation, may have tasted a little bit sweet and were therefore preferred for consumption and seed-distribution; this did initiate competitive selection: The sweeter the fruit, the more successful it became. The lovely colors of these same fruits, advertising their deliciousness and digestibility, raised the level of beauty in nature.

We cannot deny that combative behavior was often very effective in strengthening certain racial strains. The potency of this motive force becomes apparent when we examine the weapons at the disposal of vegetarian mammals. These animals have no sharp claws, no saber teeth, such as meat-eaters had to develop "professionally." Instead, rhinos and many ruminants grew horns—a feature no meat-eaters had to acquire. Horns, even in defensively oriented creatures, offer a survival advantage.

However, these weapons were not needed for procuring food. Since they were not essential, they became mere showpieces. Then aesthetic selection took over. Other organs usually obey the guideline "form follows function"; not so the ornamental horns. The more baroque and fantastic these protuberances are, the more successful they appear to be. The mainly hornless females are moved to admiration by many-branched antlers and dashingly spiraled horns. Competing males are also impressed with the menacing looks and regal bearing of the crowned champions; even fierce duels are rarely lethal, retaining an ornamental, courtly character.

In this special case we can, for once, actually prove that it is not necessarily "the fittest" who survive, that it is not the most efficient forms who are always favored by natural selection. There are occasional mutations of European deer whom foresters and hunters call *Mörderhirsche,* murderous deer: they lack the forks and ornaments of the usual antlers; instead, they carry sharply pointed, straight daggers on their skulls. The supposed Darwinian selection pressure should make these specimens victorious; and, theoretically, in a few generations they should displace the showier, aesthetically pleasing deer. The whole gestalt of the deer should be modified in the direction of a murderous model. But this has not happened. The jagged, multiple antlers remained more efficient psychologically, demanding respect from rival bucks, admiration and sexual favors from the does. The fights of many males in different species have become rituals; they are not supposed to lead to bloodletting. The convoluted spiral horns on the Kudu and other antelopes cannot even be used to gore an opponent.

How badly this high advertising budget can misfire was demonstrated by the Irish giant deer and by the North American giant elk: in their final shapes the antlers weighed as much as the entire rest of the skeleton and rested, completely useless, on the backs of their bearers. The "bad taste" in the aesthetic selection by their females decided their struggle for life in a permanently negative sense: They died out.

I suspect that mammoth and mastodon went the same way. Paleontology has not yet found a satisfactory explanation for the gigantism of teeth, horns, bizarre armor plates, and excessive body size. The neglected field of aesthetic selection might furnish some answers to these riddles.

Selection by means of sensuality can only function properly if females also assume the burden of choice. If it were always only the strongest of several competing males who carries away the prize by force, this type of friendly selection would not work at all. In older zoology books we read that the does pay hardly any attention while the bucks beat their brains out. I think that macho prejudices guided and filtered these observations. Recently, a much wider variety of sex behavior has been documented.[15]

This behavior is called "lekking," from the Swedish word *leka,* to play. An astounding range of animals has developed lek behavior, with males playing and displaying for the admiration of choosy females. Combat becomes a game. Locking their horns, Grant's gazelles joust at communal gatherings "in which individual males perform elaborate displays to attract a female for mating."[16]

Many game birds, such as European ruffs, black cocks, grouse, and capercaillie, have always been observed showing off their longest and most colorful plumage to the hens, trampling the ground, singing, and acting "childishly," as Swedish biologists say. The movements often seem choreographed, stylized in a repetitive ritual. Frogs, fish, fireflies, and other insects have also evolved such rites.

The hammerhead bats of West Africa show most distinctly that the female does the selecting for procreation in a sensual encounter. As many as 130 males hang by their feet in trees and emit metallic, honking calls. The female makes the rounds, hovering in front of this or that suitor, provoking repetitions of her favorite serenades and narrowing down her choice. "It's quite clear that in these bats the female is comparing males," says Jack Bradbury of the University of California in San Diego. The males are gentlemanly about it and don't interfere in any way.

It is by no means always the dominant male of a group who monopolizes the gene pool. Bradbury points out that the female sage grouse may solicit mating from subdominant males who are losing battles.[17]

The forces and strivings that inhabit living matter are more varied and more beneficent than what the prophets of the "all-pervasive struggle for life" like to concede.

Undeniably, peaceful, mutually advantageous cooperation provided the initial advance in plant life: primitive algae and fungi pooled their resources and abilities to form the new breed of lichens. Progress and contentment through symbiosis: this arrangement permeates the entire biosphere, from our own digestive bacteria to the friendly birds that clean vermin from the backs of pachyderms.

The symbiotic lifestyle is, in effect, indistinguishable from what humans call "altruism."

The most important case of useful symbiosis is our human relationship with domesticated animals and hybridized plants. For twelve thousand years we meant to act egotistically in order to harvest and eat our wards; and yet we created for them pacified and, on the whole, satisfying lives. Many methods of plant- and animal-breeders benefit not only us, the consumers, but also the producers themselves, the improved plants and animals. Isn't it progress in the best sense when animals are allowed to live without the unceasing fear of pursuers and of famine, and when blossoms grow more beautiful, fruits sweeter, juicier, and more fertile? Planned selection belongs in the general tendency toward refinement, exactly like its wild, natural counterpart. Homo sapiens, with his purposeful projections and actions, is, after all, still an integral part of the biosphere.

In our present era the opposing trends of cooperation and aggression are each getting stronger. This amounts to a polarization of life's various functions. Sometimes it may seem as if the good and the evil principles were mustering their forces for a decisive battle.

The "good" principle of aesthetic selection is relatively young. In the Triassic period, the ferns and coniferous trees did not develop any attractively colored parts because they did not need to attract insects: Their pollination was accomplished by the wind, and the wind does not care about beauty. But from the Tertiary period on flowers and fruits were bound to become ever more colorful, fragrant, and appetizing. This introduced beauty, properly speaking, into the world; of course flaming sunsets existed earlier, but the eye of a beholder has to exist before we can speak of aesthetic attractiveness. Beauty and cooperation have both become more widespread and more decisive in recent geological times.

Counteracting this trend, the "evil" principles have become ever more crass and destructive. Entire species have been willfully destroyed for no corresponding gain. Selection and technological progress have relied far too much on war, culminating in globe-encircling world wars and pollution.

When we compare the two main selective functions—cooperation and aggression—and put them into such an absolute and perhaps exaggerated opposition, we can have no doubt as to which of these tendencies biosophy must lend its support from now on.

Some philosophers, politicians, and eugenists, following Nietzsche's lead, consider it necessary that the most excellent individuals of a given race displace or even exterminate the inferior ones without any sentimental qualms so that the lower forms cannot procreate and swamp the race with their bad genes.

That is also the reason why some of the best biologists cling so tenaciously to the dogma that life is universal strife: They think that accidental, unfavorable mutations would permeate and destroy any species if the misfits were not weeded out by force.

The blessings of this seemingly logical theory have been mixed. In plant and animal breeding, for but very specific purposes, it has been enormously successful. In human eugenics, statecraft, and philosophical speculation it has worked as a pernicious factor. To breed a superman according to prejudicial specifications would be an extremely cruel and, in the last analysis, self-defeating undertaking. The human race is great by virtue of its variety.

But even in free, natural selection, fighting is not all-important. Most sickly and organically disadvantaged individuals are taken out of circulation by an early natural death. Whether they are eaten by predators after they have fallen back from a wandering herd, or whether they just die on the roadside—neither occurrence can possibly influence the pattern of procreation in any species. The benefit of the wolf to the flock of sheep is largely a figment of geneticists' imagination.

Besides, there is another eugenic factor often overlooked by modern biologists: To the choosy females, especially among higher animals, misfits appear ugly. In selecting a sexual partner, males and females look for "regular" individuals: weak, queer, divergent specimens are instinctively judged undesirable. Nature has given an aesthetic sense to many animals, and this sense serves to weed out the unhealthy and the monstrosities after the first generation.

It is not self-evident that sick, weak, and deformed beings should be considerd ugly. But the protective mechanism of aesthetic selection works very effectively. It amounts to a self-regulatory will to health and eugenic stability in many species. The strong, the symmetrical, the agile specimens appear aesthetically attractive to an animal choosing a sexual partner; the "born losers" usually don't have to be eliminated through combat.

Many morphological developments have been caused by love, not by hate. Love has shaped peacocks and Argus pheasants, varicolored songbirds and fish, butterflies and blossoms. Nature simply is not "red in tooth and claw"; it is decked out in beautiful living color.

Unfortunately, even the best nature films and television documentaries show a bias toward violence. The normal quiet of a peaceful habitat would bore the average audience, so the filmmakers select combat, hunting, devouring of prey and compress these into a short time period, thereby falsifying the animal life they purport to present. Thus innumerable children and adults receive a message of unending war. But it is simply not true that life and strife must rhyme all through nature's realm.

Darwinists have the bad habit of talking about the "struggle for existence" even when they mean only peaceful emulation. Of course the lion never lay down with the lamb, and the tales of an earthly paradise give us only a symbolic insight into our subconscious longings. However, there are instances of paradisiacal eco-systems on secluded islands. When the sea shut out all large preda-tors, the local bird populations—contrary to the prevalent genetic theory—did not degenerate at all. Instead they developed into multiple racial strains that are aesthetically superior to their rela-tives on the mainland. Some trail long, glittering banners through the peaceful forests; some develop the most intricate courtship pat-terns. To our puritanical biologists, such lovely developments ap-pear as dead-end streets and useless digressions from the efficient business of living; a philosophically untenable position.

It is impossible to understand certain phenomena in the bio-sphere if you deny that aesthetic selection is at work. Some scien-tists are so used to acknowledging only force as the selective factor that they have to resort to the strangest hypotheses to discover an "unaesthetic" purpose in, for example, the sound production of songbirds. What tortured arguments some zoologists have thought up to elucidate why birds sing—something perfectly clear to any naive nature lover! One scientist explains that birds in soli-tary confinement keep singing for hours on end because they are bored. Could it not be that the imprisoned bird hopes vaguely to attract sympathetic comrades or a female by his song of longing? And how should boredom explain similar outpourings in the free forest?

The modern zoological explanation of birdsong is territorial: a male bird is supposed to sing in order to indicate that his realm extends as far as his voice and that no rival from his own species should approach his feeding ground and his female. Yet in Califor-nia I have often observed male mockingbirds exchanging their perches on neighboring trees—singing their lively songs without interruption even while flying to each other's place on the branches. Occasionally, in early spring, they produce short, ugly warning cries that suffice to turn away prospective competitors. When these same birds wish to bother one of my cats, they have shrieking "meows" at their disposal. They do not use their flute-like song as a deterrent.

Caged birds sing even longer hours than free ones. How does this jibe with the theory that birdsong only marks a territory? Can a bird in a cage possibly feel more menaced by intruders than it would in bushes or a tree?

Why do nightingales and mockingbirds sing all through the night, why does the lark flutter trilling high through the morning sky without paying attention to the plot of ground from which it ascended? Primarily, birds have fun producing beautiful melodies. And of course the male wants to seduce his female, thus—coincidentally—transmitting his special gift to his progeny. If we allow the songbirds to spend a few more millennia on this earth, their songs will, no doubt, become even more beautiful (both to their mates and, if people happen to be still around, to human ears).

Behind the denial of an aesthetic sense in animals lurks the old hubris of homo sapiens. We think that only we are able to produce and appreciate beauty, and that other creatures are too stupid for these higher functions.

No being, not even a human one, produces beauty as such. Artists make pictures, statues, music; architects erect buildings; artisans manufacture chairs: they hope that their products will please and attract other people. A potter does not make beauty, but a pot. Aesthetic quality often appears overwhelmingly real, but it exists solely in the subject's relation to the object. It is a function of life, ergo relative to life. Even inanimate beauty—a rainbow, a sunrise—comes into being only if someone sees it. Beauty is a most fragile miracle.

This observation is not changed by the fact that sometimes the general public becomes enamored with certain kinds of art; then even prosaic financiers consider aesthetic value a stable enough commodity in which to invest money, and then only can beauty be expressed in figures. Usually, however, aesthetic values resist quantification and statistical endeavors, and that makes them unfit for exact science.

The starling is satisfied when his spouse likes his song; the aesthetician is not. Volumes upon volumes have been written about the antinomies of taste, about realism or idealism concerning values, about definitions of beauty; and speculation about these matters will not end so long as one creature admires a product of another, which it cannot produce itself. Suffice it to state that beauty, though existing only relative to a beholder, yet shows some surprising constants, some rules, some common features in widely differing phenomena.

It is quite striking to note that most long, drawn-out sound productions of animals appear equally attractive to us humans. A crow would be ashamed to emit sustained cawing for hours, as nightingale and lark sustain their song. The crow's voice emissions, even if expressive, don't serve the purpose of influencing other beings by aesthetic charm; I'm reasonably sure that neither the crow nor the seagull feels aesthetic pleasure while shrieking. Cries of warning, of covetousness, of provocation sound differently from wooing calls; one cannot be mistaken for the other. The croaking of a male frog drives other male frogs away: This has been observed. The song of the blackbird, on the contrary, wants to attract, not to repulse.

If it were true that birdsong serves to stake out the male bird's territorial claim and to drive away intruders, the ugliest and most menacing tune should be the most successful. By selection through the generations, the sounds of the jealous and grabby male bird should be metamorphosed into hissing, cackling, and scolding sounds; and the inefficiently sweet, attractive melodies of nightingale and thrush should by now have been muted all over the earth.

It is an interesting and not at all self-evident fact that many specific animal sounds are also convincing to other races. If there were no widespread aesthetic agreement, why would the snake, the goose, and the leopard hiss for repulsion? The vocabulary is instinctively clear to a wide variety of species. When my cat wants to flatter me or to obtain milk, he does not use his word "hiss," but "eeooo." For aggressive purposes he never uses the conciliatory-sounding "miaow," but a spitting noise. When a quail calls its chicks it sounds to me like "come come come." And when mockingbirds sing, they have in mind beauty and zest for life. I cannot ask them about this, but I can observe their parallel motion. There is, of course, a chance for fatal mix-ups and switches; but empathy is usually a rather reliable way to understanding.

There are hardly any ugly sustained noises in nature. Warning signals and angry exclamations are of short duration only, in keeping with their purpose. Crickets, with their marathon chirping, serve love—they may enjoy their own fiddling, even if they don't give us the purest artistic enjoyment. Occasionally, a coyote howls plaintively through the night; but generally the agreeable sounds are prevalent.

Ugly noises, where they occur on the globe, are usually generated by human beings. Industrial racket, traffic noise, military hate songs, marching boots, and the thunder of guns: We really should not presume that we have monopolized aesthetics!

A nightingale knows that he has pleasing melodies at his disposal, and he uses this gift for self-enjoyment as well as for the admiration of others. We should appreciate birdsong without falsifying it by restrictive utilitarian theories. Why should we add philosophical pollution to our other misdeeds?

The formula "survival of the fittest" has often been criticized. Invented by Herbert Spencer, hesitatingly adopted by Darwin, it has caused more confusion than clarification. It contains a circular conclusion: Who survives? The fittest. Who is the fittest? The one who survives. Value standards that would sustain this formulation would have to be absolute in order to be normative, but absolute judgments usually lead to dogmas and to intolerance.

As a loose description of facts in nature that formula is sometimes useful, sometimes misleading, and often downright false. Instead of generalizing the survival of the fittest we should observe and accept the frequent *survival of the fanciest*. The prevalence of the most attractive creatures became a complementary inheritance law during the Tertiary and Quaternary eras.

Not every being glorying in its own beauty is automatically pounced upon and eaten. Attractiveness does not necessarily mean attractiveness to enemies.

Inconspicuous adaptations to surrounding colors and shapes amaze us because they are not the general rule. An owl resembling a tree trunk, a mantis mimicking a leafy twig, a snow rabbit putting on its winter costume seem remarkably ingenious to us—as rarities.

Mimicry would have spread among many more living things if life depended only on eating and not also on loving. Every higher-organized animal in its mating age must send out waves of odors, enticing calls, color orgies: promises of future happiness or, putting it more soberly, signals of an attractive kind. And if these emanations of propaganda don't always seem beautiful to us humans, they must appear so to the concerned members of the same species. Whenever one creature needs another living being—the blossom the butterfly, the songbird his mate—it must broadcast distinct messages into the wide world. The will to symbiosis directly counteracts the spreading of mimicry.

Thus the biological pendulum swings between utility and beauty, always trying to settle into a new balance. And thus life always renews itself and becomes interesting. Grey boredom, timid hide-and-seek, endless combat cannot monopolize life—and, unfortunately, neither can love.

In my garden in California I have often observed that hummingbirds select the showiest hibiscus blossoms in order to slake their thirst for nectar. I like to think that a feedback is arising from this preference. The females, schooled to look for the most colorful flowers, will then also look for the most glittering male birds. Flower-colored butterflies prefer each other because they have been trained by the luminous petals to seek satisfaction near multicolored signals. This natural training produces ever more glorious butterflies and hummingbirds, and the world becomes a little lovelier.

Is this perhaps the explanation for the incredibly naturalistic designs of water drops on butterfly wings? A liquid drop, even if only an illusory one, may seem so attractive to the eyes of the little animal that it prefers that sexual partner who provides the illusion of offering to quench the visitor's thirst.

My mother used to quote a proverb in her earthy *plattdeutsch* (Low German) dialect *"Wat dem eenen sin uul, is dem annern sin nachtigall."* ("One man's owl is another man's nightingale.") And then there is the old French analysis of aesthetic relativity: *"Qui du cul d'un chien tombe amourose, il lui paraît une rose."* ("If you fall in love with a dog's arse, it will seem a rose to you.")

Admittedly, an owl finds the hooting of another owl more charming than the nightingale's song. We also know that the smell and taste of a rotting cadaver has an overpowering attraction for certain flies. One African flower has even developed the exact smell of decomposing flesh in order to attract the gravedigger insects for the paradoxical purpose of life's renewal by pollination: a very successful deception. A few more plants—a morel, among others—have developed the same attraction through stinking. But, again, we must not overemphasize this relativity of taste; the attractive stinkers are a tiny minority.

On the other hand: that substance which serves as no other in nature to allure animals—namely, honey—seems desirable to a wide variety of palates. The sweet drink that was "invented" for the purpose of enticing insects is also craved by such divergent animals as bears, hummingbirds, and humans; this proves that honey must have an objectively high place on any taste scale. There must be a widespread pragmatic agreement about aesthetic preferences. Statistically, at least, we can state that sweet is better than sour.

During a more romantic age, such valuations were accepted as a matter of course. Today's scientific investigations leave these facts aside because of a remnant of puritanism. Beauty is not dignified enough. Just as the Protestant ethic frowned on dancing and threw the statues of saints out of the churches, contemporary science would think it frivolous to put such a luxury item as beauty into its formulae. Some scientists seem to be plagued by a bad conscience if they cannot avoid including beautiful phenomena in their sober descriptions. Lorenz quotes the jocular, but somewhat frightening, remark of his teacher, Oskar Heinroth: "Next to the wings of the Argus pheasant, the hectic life of Western civilized man is the most stupid product of intra-specific selection."[18] Let's look without prejudice at the gorgeous wooing display of the Argus pheasant, his umbrella-like wings fanning out and revealing about four hundred regularly distributed, artfully shaded eyelike designs: How can we possibly designate this as a blunder of evolution, or even as organically inferior? It is indeed a crowning achievement of sexual selection, and it fulfills its purpose to stimulate the Argus hen's love; is this not enough? The preconceived derogation of luxurious beauty must be deeply ingrained. Lorenz asserts: "Wherever competition between members of a species effects sexual selection, there is grave danger that members of a species may in demented competition drive each other into the most stupid blind alley of evolution."[19]

I protest. We call human breeders of long-tailed goldfish and multicolored pigeons intelligent; why, then, should natural evolution, accomplishing similar feats on pheasants and parrots, be singled out as stupid? Lavish ostentation and adornment did not prevent these animals from being remarkably "fit" for their own surroundings. In contrast, many inconspicuous, grey, matter-of-factly built life forms have died out. Beauty is definitely not a handicap.

Behavioral physiology has done much to elucidate the role of aggression. But how can science hope to defuse the "war of all against all," at least in theory, if it has a blind spot for beauty and its desirability? We have to recognize aesthetic value as a legitimate aim of developing species and of each individual.

Human beings have an incomparably wider latitude of taste than the other creatures. The hummingbird can live only on nectar. It could not exist if some flowers had not developed a special access mechanism for its particular beak. The silkworm eats only mulberry leaves, it dies of hunger if you put it on any other bush or tree. The koala bear relishes eucalyptus leaves exclusively, the anteater likes nothing but ants. Chimpanzees have a more catholic taste. They usually eat fruits and juicy greenery; periodically, however, overcome by fleshly desire, they may rip a baboon baby to pieces and distribute it among their tribe.

Our own predilections and digestive faculties are not confined to any ecological niche. Many Mexicans live largely on beans and corn; Eskimos are nourished by seal meat, oil, and fish: No greater variety in the feeding habits of one single species is imaginable. This entails vastly divergent taste preferences in other fields besides food, and produces contradictory value judgments. One person enjoys blubber, another one beans. One abhors pork, another refuses any meat whatsoever, a third despises all raw vegetables. This wide latitude is also reflected in our concepts of beauty. We should be glad that our ethical and aesthetic preferences have some basic congruity, and acknowledge our differences with a smile. A multifarious being like homo sapiens should adopt tolerance as "second nature," in the truest sense.

We have seen in what manner life wants to refine itself. We have followed the genetic process of aesthetic selection, by means of which more beautiful forms are developed among plants and animals; flowers and fruits, butterflies and fish, herons and ducks and baboons appear ever more colorful and ornate. We have tried to show that sexual selection is frequently the motor for this aesthetic progress. In other words: Love influences the evolution of many races in a practical, unpoetic way—with, if you will, poetic results. Without selective, even finicky erotic tastes there would hardly be any embellishment, no consideration, no chivalric, ritualized forms of living together. And this progress then reflects back on love's refinement. Human eroticism is more sensitive, more complicated, more spiritually satisfying than the sexuality of worms, fish, and frogs.

What makes the difference? The most striking innovation is tenderness. The higher up we look on the genealogical tree of life, the more clearly we see this refinement. It leads from the unfeeling fertilization of conifers to the bodily separated spawning of fish, to the crude jumping and squeezing of lower quadrupeds, to the courtship dances of birds, and finally to the complicated erotic customs of human beings. How did this finesse arise?

In the warm-blooded birds and mammals, love always has something to do with warmth. "She felt a warm longing"—"a red-hot lover": in prose and poetry the connection is clearly indicated.

Embracing is an agreeable feeling to warm-blooded beings because it reduces the loss of hard-gained body warmth. This starts with mother love. The chick under the hen's wing, the kangaroo baby in the pouch need less internal heating, less oxygen, and less food intake to mature in the lazy peace of warm motherly protection. The fledgling saves energy; consequently, its skin nerves are conditioned to find sympathetic touch attractive. The young lovers who walk wrapped in a tight embrace through a cold park don't care about this economic transference; to them the love experience appears cosmic, transcendental, unexplainable. And this is as it should be.

What is the basic advantage of being warm-blooded? Why has life, through millions of years, perfected this expensive complication?

Chemical reactions take place a little more speedily when the solutions are warmed up. Nutritional materials dissolve faster in the stomach acid if the digestive tract is heated; the bloodstream takes them up faster if it is warm; circulation, utilization, and elimination proceed at a more efficient pace; the body mechanism can develop more results in a given amount of time, even thought processes will be more flexible and fluent in a warm brain.

Love is not a cosmic phenomenon. It is only possible between the freezing and boiling points of water. All earthly life processes known to us depend on chemical transmutations that are possible only in watery solution. God Eros himself is dependent on temperature.

It is not a sacrilege to reduce such noble phenomena as tenderness and motherly love to physical processes. It is precisely this great unity of physical, chemical, mental, spiritual things which gives up hope for our future development and for the salvation of humanity from the orgies of hatred during wars.

In order to continue living with a certain degree of optimism we must pin our hopes on Eros, the power to which Sigmund Freud assigned the task of counteracting the aggressive drive. Luckily, we are warm-blooded organisms—not too cold, not too hot, we possess a warm heart. Warm-blooded creatures know forms of "togetherness" unknown in earlier geological periods. Nonerotic

fondling occurs only among birds and mammals. Finches sit tight-
ly cuddled on a twig in the wintry air, monkeys love close contact.
And this closeness is also natural to brothers, sisters, and friends,
not only to lovers.

This magnetism is countermanded by our individualism, by our
joy in free mobility. The drive toward territorial possession and
exclusivity, the need for privacy—which is already strong in lower
life forms—leads to the well-defined distance each individual
wants to establish between itself and its nearest neighbor.
Nonetheless, humans have always tended to assemble in caves or
groves and to crowd together in settlements. The tendency toward
agglomeration initiated the formation of communities and nations,
and perhaps all of humanity will learn to see the advantages that
can be gained by cohesion—or, to choose a "warmer" term, by
love of neighbor. Then the specters of senseless, cold aggresssion
will dissolve in laughter.

If we thus accept love as one of the strongest motive powers of
evolution, the question arises: Where will this development lead
life? If left to its own devices, natural evolution will lead to increased peaceful cooperation. When a principle proves as useful as
love has since time immemorial, nature would be quite perverse to
negate this force instead of enhancing it. This entails a rather surprising discovery: Such modern trends as pacifism, vegetarianism,
economic cooperation and overall planning, courts of international
justice and the United Nations point in the direction of the general
biological progress.

We should recognize that this supra-ordinated natural development gives us certain duties and rights. The dogma "Life is war of
all against all" made pacifists feel that their endeavors were anti-
natural. "Life is also cooperation": This sentence can give the
peacemakers a very good conscience indeed.

Exact scientists usually shun those higher concepts that seem to
many of them to be merely "romanticizing commonplaces." Even
though biologists have to deal with cumulative complications and

with aesthetic and spiritual progressions, they are reticent about philosophical generalizations. This is justified as long as it does not cause a denial of certain observable tendencies and serial phenomena.

Julian Huxley describes the history of horses, the improvement in their limb structure, their brain power, and the grinding machinery of their teeth. But he warns his readers that

improvement is not yet a generally recognized technical term in biology. In fact, I should imagine that many of my biological colleagues would jib at its use. Some would shy away from it because it sounded teleological, while others would say that it implied a judgment of value, and that value judgments were not scientific, or at least were outside the purview of science. However, living things *are* improved during evolution, and we need a term to denote that fact, and to crystallize our ideas about it.[20]

The formula "life for life's sake" can be a guide to a better future if we subsume the concept of improvement under the concept of life. The result: genuine, intelligent, and aesthetic progress.

It would be nice if we could rely on natural selection to rid us of our superfluous warrior instincts. If the warriors among us would kill each other off, thereby demonstrating their "unfitness" for higher forms of life, everything would be all right. Unfortunately, the fighters have a tendency to destroy more peaceable women and children than aggressive males; thus the inheritable genes won't become more pacifistic.

The overriding urgency of a pacification program for humankind is felt by many. Suggestions are being made as to how the warrior-like "nature" of man can be changed. Some reformers even want to add female hormones to our drinking water in order to make males less aggressive.

Eunuchs are not aggressive; but who would voluntarily prefer a eunuch's lifestyle? *Blind men don't shoot. Should we therefore rid ourselves of our eyesight?*

All this is certainly not necessary. The intelligence we have already developed, coupled with our capacity for learning, should easily master the task of avoiding catastrophic quarrels. Homo sapiens now has sufficient reserves of cooperative spirit, enough capacity for selflessness and even for self-sacrifice to prevent future bloodletting and to guide incipient brawls into formalized channels. It must be possible that we remain proud, active people, directing our aggression against hunger and sickness and corruption in the world.

Not so very long ago, people felt pleasure in watching killings: They came from far and wide to thrill at executions on gallows and guillotine. We have changed. We don't like live brutality any more—we prefer it in the movies, where blood isn't wet. It's a question of improved taste. Aesthetic endeavors, once considered sissifying, become essential for our survival. Is it not a wonderful coincidence that these trends agree exactly with the most general biological development? Life has an immanent vector toward aesthetic improvement.

Only human beings have not yet become full-fledged members of the natural improvement society. We put smoke-belching factories and slums into the landscape, we damage the biosphere with garbage, strip mining, and war. Did we receive the most developed brains for this purpose? Many warm-hearted and farseeing men and women combat this devaluation. As early as 1802 William Blake wished we would replace the "dark satanic mills" with a new Jerusalem. The visionary must be recognized today as eminently practical.

We must extend that progress, which appeared so pervasive in biological development, into the future—for life's sake.

3. The Nonsense of Human History

"All roads lead to Rome," said the Roman, and promptly left for other destinations: into the blue, into the blood-red.

The worst penalty the Greek gods could devise for the rebellious Sisyphus was uselessness: the unending repetition of a compulsive action without the possibility of progress. Sisyphus had to push a rock up a steep mountainside, and every time he reached the top the rock escaped, rolled down again, had to be pushed up again, rolled—

But the gods forgot a simple fact: The rock, in the course of time, got used up. The sharp edges, which at first bloodied Sisyphus' hands, became smooth during the first century of his servitude. The protruding irregularities were flattened out during the next five hundred years, converting the difficult act of pushing the load into an easier rolling operation. In the next millennium the rock diminished in size, and the roadbed became more even. Finally, it could hardly be called a rock any more; only a pebble remained.

The other day Sisyphus had the idea of putting that pebble into his pocket where he carried it around, together with his happy-pills and credit cards. Now each morning he takes the elevator to the twenty-eighth floor of the office building which has sprung up on the site of his penance, and he rides it down again in the evening.

The raw material of life that has been handed down to us has astonishing qualities. The inherent will to complication has, within the span of 500 million years, magically transformed algae and amoebae into apple trees and apes. Through half a billion years life has preserved itself, has spread, has satisfied and refined itself. In spite of many setbacks and false starts, our retrospective view can discern a continuous enhancement. Biological development has indeed been a fascinating success story.

Only the last one-hundredth of this saga of progress has brought certain difficulties. Prior to that moment the proverbial observer from Sirius would have been entitled to an optimistic prognosis concerning terrestrial life's future chances. But in more recent times his crystal ball would have become clouded.

Perhaps half a million years ago one of our ancestors stood up on his hind legs and started questioning: Why should I live for life's sake—why should life not occasionally function for my sake? We know what came of this rebelliousness: wooden spears and stone axes, fire and arithmetic, hunting and war; certainly an interesting career. The improvement of our various aptitudes made us the beneficiaries of the biosphere, eliminating our untameable competitors and using our dumb friends for our own domestic ends.

For approximately the last five thousand years, this special development has merited the name "history." Is this history still the continuation of the original biological progression? Or have the principles been changed?

All our actions make sense only in relation to our human-ness, to our biological constitution and needs. As Friedrich Schiller said: "Nature maintains the machinery of life through hunger and love." All our motivations depend on our hominitude, so to speak. Celestial spheres and subatomic particles do not know love, hate, pain, or pleasure—and, consequently, they have no comedies or tragedies. Sun and moon, treated in most languages as masculine and feminine, actually have no sex whatsoever; and the antique concept of an animated, sexually organized cosmos with jealous planets, lovesick river nymphs, and lustful winds was nothing but superstition. We, the living, stand completely alone with our petty hates, with noble love and diabolical sadism, and with our hyperbolic ambition. All these are functions of nerves and glands, not independent forces. A meteor burning up in the atmosphere knows no pain and therefore cannot rouse anybody's pity. Smiling benevolently, an innocent youth can pick a flower and hand it to his sweetheart: he does not suppose that this broken flower could feel hurt. The modern botanist is certain that the pine tree broadcasting its spores to the wind derives no pleasurable sentiments from this sex act; love, as an incentive to fertilization, simply is not needed among pines.

"Heavenly" bliss, "eternal" regret? These are similes, nothing else. Even when we transform marble, parchment, and film into our witnesses, we don't escape from the organic sphere: without human beings there is no art, no justice, no wisdom.

Once you have accepted this condition, you can look at world history in a more modest way, namely, as human history. So-called world-shaking events such as the conquests of Alexander or Cortez are, as physical movements, less displacing than a medium-sized volcanic eruption. This is one possible perspective: seen mechanistically, our highest feelings and deepest thoughts are just brainwaves, approximately twenty watts strong in each individual. This is, of course, not an inadequate point of view to apply to mighty philosophical thought or the enormous currents of history; but it serves to dampen our all too high-flung speculations.

We can never depict to ourselves anything ultra-human without referring back to sensual models. Even while integrating the auxiliary thinking of mathematics and computer technique into the workings of our mind, we remain bound to the world of our senses. A sphere appears to our inner eye as a circle. When we observe a ball turning around, we clearly perceive that there is no circle drawn on its surface; but this does not destroy our illusion. When we sketch the ball on a flat surface, we naturally draw a circle. When we face the sea or a meadow our visual field is cut in half by a horizontal line, and we cannot shed this impression in spite of our knowledge that there is no straight line out there in the landscape. And when we see two rocks clashing, we feel a twitching pain deep inside. Intellectually, we discard the feeling almost before it becomes conscious; but the sensation remains.

Human-ness is our life element, and therefore our history does not unfold in a sublime, logical way, abiding by the laws of nature and of theoretical ethics. History has our own flaws, it functions by rapaciousness and sentimentality, by stupidity and vanity, and by our sometimes ridiculous, sometimes truly grandiose striving for unattainable goals.

We can observe human history in the same cool and unimpassioned manner we use to observe barnyard fowl or the denizens of an aquarium. Paradoxically speaking: To view historic phenomena as unreasonable manifestations of life gives them the most reasonable appearance.

We can then appreciate the historic role of, for example, the *pecking order,* seeing its laws and workings in the largest human context. We use the image to effectively organize an army, a barnyard population, or a commercial firm. The rooster bites the wattles of the oldest or strongest hen who, shaking her head in mild disapproval, accepts his authority. This hen then pecks a weaker sister; that one submits without protest, but vents her resentment on a still weaker bird; and so on. Finally, a poor, ugly, ragged, always hungry animal, clinging to walls and fences, is defined as the lowest member of the social order. Newly arriving individuals find their place after a few probes and soon will no longer doubt the "natural" order. Revolts and upheavals occur only after external changes, when the entire milieu has become questionable. The pecking process is not intelligent, but it is effective.

The uppermost specimens of the human pecking order used to imagine that they were descended from certain gods or that they had blue blood in their veins—qualities that were never proved objectively but which, through centuries, acquired a frightening reality.

A similar, purely biological force is *territoriality.* Many otherwise dissimilar species have the instinctive or customary urge to divide an available area into territories that then will be defended by the mature males against usurpers and competitors. In both animals and plants this will to dominate territory usually guarantees feeding and nesting privacy for an optimal number of families.

Yet when humans evince the same primitive urges, they embellish them with talk about god-given rights. They even believe that a plot of land is, in some mystical fashion, soaked through with one certain national character. Property rights applied to the soil are felt by the species homo sapiens to be much more absolute than some other claims and needs which, in our modern situation, would appear incomparably more important.

The most nefarious pre-human behavior pattern, which shaped much of our history, is the *bellwether mentality*, formerly called the *Führer principle*. If a strong male individual is convinced of his own infalliability, families, tribes, and entire peoples will tend to follow him unquestioningly. Usually, this specimen must be an unsavory character in order to be effective. The seductions of unchecked power are the one thing he cannot conquer.

Perhaps the most dangerous of these inherited animalisms is the *stampede*. Crowd movements, both human and animal, allow no individualistic hesitation or deviation; and, by sheer momentum, they sweep away all normal inhibitions. Cattle or lemmings, once set in motion, disregard self-destruction. The concerted vector of an army in the field, just like the meanderings of a school of fish or the migratory drive of birds of passage, cannot tolerate singular exceptions and separation from the crowd. Many human mass movements and wars bear the same terrifying characteristics. Dissent during such times seems organically impossible. The few dissidents are almost automatically designated as traitors or cowards by the inebriated groups—until, many years later, they may be recognized as saints.

Parallels between biology and history make more sense than the motives which the actors on the political stage believe to be operative. The human grounds for historic actions, as proclaimed by the participants themselves, are often unbelievably absurd.

Thus some bold monk fells a sacred oak tree dedicated to the god Wotan; and because no lightning bolt slays the perpetrator, an entire tribe accepts Christianity. Nobody makes a control experiment, such as sticking a pin through the holy Host that was believed to bleed from such treatment. The avoidance of verification in this case is lauded as faith, whereas all earlier trustful acceptances are condemned as superstition. Entire populations and religions become divided by such nonessential preferences as whether Friday, Saturday, or Sunday should be the sanctified day of rest.

The simple biological fact of *adult male grouchiness,* common to many beasts and man, has exercised a tremendous influence on the course of history. The slogan *Ceterum censeo Carthaginem esse delendam* ("Furthermore, I vote that Carthage must be destroyed"), repeated without factual elaboration by an obstinate senator at the end of each speech, finally destroyed the oriental branch of Mediterranean culture. It sounds learned to make economic reasons responsible for the forays of the Huns or for the Crusades; but without the harsh male character and its penchant for conquest they would not have taken place. The good or bad mood of a prince or a pope, an erotic infatuation, or a personal vendetta have effected worldwide power shifts. Pieces of multicolored cloth have guided murderous multitudes. Hypnotic symbols such as Mohammed's moon sickle on a green banner, the cross-shaped sword, and the swastika were carried through the world, leaving heaps of corpses behind. Abstruse theological disputes—whether the Eucharistic wafer is or merely signifies the body of Christ, whether the cow is sacred or edible—have torn populations apart. Escutcheons like the red and the white rose, family loyalties, forged claims to inheritances have caused wars and civil wars. Somebody one fine day felt called upon to take vengeance for some deed that had occurred a hundred times without any consequences; and from this vengeful mood whole nations were annihilated.

Every political movement has to keep going, just like a bicycle that falls over helplessly when it is not pedaled: Only constant motion supports it. As long as a vital urge propels a political entity, it seems to embody all sense and all purpose—to its members at least. Nothing appears more important—for a while—than to subject the whole world to the pope or the sultan, to the emperor or to the dictatorship of the proletariat. An era demands with overriding urgency to technicize or commercialize nature; to establish a ranking order among races; to chase sin from the world. Any person not hypnotized by such broad purposes feels strangely excluded from salvation and is considered a traitor—until the mood of the masses, or their leadership, changes and the former "sense of life" seems unreal.

The sense of life does not belong to the domain of intellect; the way to this sense, however, does.

One human activity, which some historians consider the most contrary to nature, occurred during Roman banquets: A patrician would interrupt his gluttonous feast only to have a slave tickle the inside of his throat, whereupon he would empty his stomach and continue his eating and drinking.

But nature offers some examples of gluttony that put the Roman aristocrats to shame. When certain sharks get into a school of herring, they eat and eat until they vomit thousands of killed herring, whereupon they go on eating.

One particular dragonfly larva is perhaps the most uninhibited devourer. The moment it leaves the egg at the pond's bottom it eats its weaker sisters and every other obtainable animal. Slowly it eats its way up toward the surface, for it too strives after higher things. Above the surface it bursts, unfolds its wings, and never pauses in its meal. This lovely insect has been observed to ingest forty-two flies within two hours without becoming less hungry. If you hold its own tail in front of its mouth, it eats itself; and this, to be sure, is its final (not to say just) dessert.

If we disapprove of such behavior, should we really call Alexander "the Great"? Plutarch reports: "Alexander wept when he heard from Anaxarchus that there exist an unlimited number of worlds. Alexander explained: Is it not lamentable that, if there are so many worlds, we have not yet conquered even one?"

Why are people so good at being bad—and so bad at being good?

No doubt: entire cultures were erected on false grounds. The blood sacrifice of the firstborn son to assuage the possible wrath of imagined deities was a sorry custom, but many fertile communities survived this and similar bloodlettings. Some tribes kill their newborn twins: Multiple births are considered a bad omen. People have willingly submitted to such crude forms of population control, as they do to all kinds of tortures and inconveniences. Painful tattooing and circumcision, chastity belts made out of iron or iron-clad ethical precepts, nose rings and lip plugs, frozen monogamy, habitual murder of all shipwrecked strangers—the individual suffered, but the state became, through compliance of its members, ever stronger.

Sometimes we have come up with excellent inventions but have not known how to use them. The ancient Chinese had gunpowder long before the Western soldiers; but, perhaps wisely, they used this propellant only for merry fireworks and rockets. Had they developed rockets with warheads, we might all today live by Lao Tse's teachings—which might not be so bad, after all.

Another case in point is the early use of the wheel. Wagons were built in Babylon three thousand years before Christ, and improved models brought power in turn to the Egyptians, Indo-Iranians, and Greeks. Yet the same invention, made independently in Mexico and not employed to full advantage, did not help the Aztecs a bit.

Diego Rivera has depicted the ancient market square of Tlatelolco on a powerful mural. In the background is a temple, in front of it are the stands of herb vendors and dog butchers, medicine men and tattooed whores. In the foreground is a little toy: a baked–clay dog on four wheels. This toy, as excavations have proved, was actually the only application which that complex civilization could find for the invention of the wheel.

Our use of atomic explosions and military rocketry may some day be viewed by later generations with the same wistful, sad smile with which we regard that Mexican toy.

Could it be that the haughty designation "homo sapiens" is not altogether justified?

Through centuries people chased after chimeras. They wasted

immense amounts of energy, which they could have used to better their circumstances. Enthralled by illusions, they erected taboos that never brought them any spiritual or material profit. The enforcement of these taboos must have consumed herculean labors.

Many local taboos—dietary laws, clothing habits, incantations, and the like—may be considered irrational in the next valley or country. None have spread around the world, even though the concerned tribes usually opined that they should. Yet some taboos have been enforced in such a general manner all over the globe that compliance is often felt to be identical with the state of being civilized.

The prohibitions against incest and cannibalism—perhaps the most rigorously enforced taboos—demonstrate clearly that we can make incredible efforts to realize something absolute: we can change the supposedly immutable human nature. Social habits, even primal urges can be modified! If we would discard warlike aggression or unlimited acquisitiveness with similarly energetic purposefulness, we would be a happier race.

Surely it was a historic mistake to forbid cannibalism. We would not plan or condone large wars if our habits would force us to eat the mountains of corpses produced by such enterprises. Is it perhaps nobler to kill the enemy and to put his nutritionally valuable flesh into the ground than to eat him with relish and the good conscience that comes from having had a valid reason to kill him? What is so humane about the disgusting spectacle of armies starving between heaps of rotting carcasses?

An old cannibal on Borneo once asked the anthropologist Bronislaw Malinowski to explain to him the "civilized" First World War. The old man did not understand how the Europeans could eat so much meat. When Malinowski explained that white people bury their dead enemies, the "savage" shook his head: "What barbarians you are to kill without a reason!"

This supposedly civilizing taboo is definitely counterproductive in the age of the atom bomb. If we—qua species homo sapiens—would have remained cannibalistic, we would instinctively refrain from making our food supply inedible through the use of poison gases and radiation. A rational, hygienically organized form of cannibalism would have become a blessing for humanity.

Demonstrably, humankind can rid itself of some of its worst habits. The history of dueling justifies this optimistic estimation. Great literature, from Shakespeare to the Russian and French novels of the late nineteenth century, is replete with duels whose fateful inevitability thrills us today. In spite of this, a contemporary character who wanted to fight a duel because of a slap on the cheek would not be heroic but ridiculous.

The problem of the duel was not a minor side issue of society. Not only fops, but some of the brightest writers and statesmen thus sacrificed their lives. Schopenhauer inveighs against this false concept of honor: "That oppression should be lifted from the higher classes which arises from the rule that anybody, at any moment, can become responsible for the whim of another crude, rough, stupid or malevolent person. It is shameful, yea crying to heaven, that two young inexperienced hotheads who exchange angry words should pay for this with their blood, health, or lives."

Nowadays, an insult does not require combat: a change of mores Schopenhauer would hardly have hoped for. Are fewer slaps being given? Perhaps. Is there less adultery? Certainly not. Only the ways of reacting have changed. We are not Pavlovian dogs who salivate every time a little bell rings.

Our cerebrum is a powerful and subtle instrument, one of whose functions it is to control and, if need be, to modify our automatic reflexes, instincts, and affects. Are these controls unnatural? Since Sigmund Freud's and Wilhelm Reich's days, many psychologists and educators have feared that the cultural checks on the free flow of our drives toward fulfillment give rise to inhibitions, complexes, neuroses—complications that may later prove to be more dangerous and destructive than the original drives. Much of this is true; but the world situation today is so precarious that we urgently need certain inhibitions—for instance, inhibitions against final solutions by using the atom bomb.

The main objection against completely uninhibited behavior is this: The cortex of our cerebrum, with its intellectual functions, was developed by nature, exactly as were the more primitive layers of our personality. The typical human brain is not a cold, rigid product of some laboratory; it has grown as a living organ. It has been developed for life's sake.

Dionysiac, "spaced-out" states of mind or non-mind probably should have their place in any person's life. From the most sublime artistic inspiration down to the most banal carnival there are, again and again, situations in which the intellect has to be switched off. But who wants to celebrate carnival all year round? Orphic mysteries and orgiastic festivals were always bound to very definite, prescribed dates of the yearly cycle—which proves that they were not purely irrational outbursts. The human control mechanisms were only turned off for certain circumscribed purposes. When there was no other inhibition, the restriction of time was still operative, and Ash Wednesday always came around "naturally."

Since we were obviously able to regulate the orgies of love, we should also be able to subordinate the orgies of hate to our intelligent will.

Can we learn something about our present and future from studying the past? Can we project the chances of our descendants in certain fields by extrapolating historical developments?

This is an old bone of contention among writers. Goethe had a completely negative attitude: "I have not grown this old," he grumped to Chancellor von Müller, "to concern myself with world history, which is the greatest absurdity there is." Having read four volumes of the history of the Hohenstaufen dynasty, he said that he had "gained nothing except the conviction that things were then even worse than now. World history is, for the higher thinker, only a web of nonsense, and little can be learned from it."

The historian Jacob Burckhardt had the opposite opinion. He found it "a magnificent spectacle to follow the spirit of mankind who, floating above all these manifestations and yet interwoven with them, builds itself a new dwelling."

Perhaps this contradiction can be resolved. If we consider history as a series of territorial losses and gains, of groups splitting up, of state treaties and broken contracts, of the rise and decay of ruling castes, the result is indeed a senseless whirling about of opposing forces that cancel each other out without ever producing permanent results.

However, if we perceive the cathedrals, the music, the literary achievements of varying periods, we can feel the radiance and fascination of history. The wars, changing political borders, ruling dynasties then become background figurations setting off the perspective into the spirituality of the past.

When we include the developing value scales of cultural history, we can discern distinct directions. The founding of successive empires adds up to nothing; but institutions of health services have built on each other. Astronomy, world traffic, chemistry became steadily more efficient. Judged according to their own principles and aims, products of the human spirit show a phenomenal progress that simply cannot be denied.

There are grounds for hoping that the directedness of cultural history will, during the coming centuries, overflow into the self-contradictory political history and carry it along.

The historian lives forward and thinks backward. Like ice floes in a wild, foggy stream, his material is irretrievably swept away. How many causes of vast historical events will forever remain unknown to us?

Enormous realignments have sometimes followed from insignificant, even ridiculous causes. Certainly the yearnings for freedom and justice often were mighty motives for social and economic upheavals. But these high ideals, in other contexts, remained ineffective for centuries. Petty motivations—jealousies inside a bureaucracy, the skill of an otherwise mediocre official in using the levers of power—were more decisive. The most frequent cause of bloody turmoil was the extinction of a ruling family without previously clarified rights of succession; and, in these cases, not even the most idealistic historian can pretend that events followed a philosophically acceptable scheme.

If the overall drift of an epoch led to unsolvable antagonisms, war seemed natural; and yet, sometimes nations resisted the strongest provocations and preserved peace. At other times one little offense acted like a spark in a gunpowder barrel.

Heinrich von Kleist, a writer who knew how to put overwhelmingly strong historical actions onto the stage, also knew about the effectiveness of tiny, insignificant details. He described how King Louis XVI of France sent a master of ceremonies to the assembled representatives of the people to order them to go home. "Perhaps it was the doubtful twist of an upper lip, or an uncertain finger play on a lace cuff which caused the fall of the French order. We read that Mirabeau stood up as soon as the master of ceremonies had departed, and proposed that the men who were present should constitute themselves right away as national assembly, and as sacrosanct."

One thing is certain: the cosmos does not care about human history. Earlier centuries had a different opinion: They thought that an earthly ruler governed not only human matters, but was mandated, protected, or menaced by supernatural powers. Thus Charlemagne's biographer, Einhard, wrote: "Very many presages announced his coming end, a fact which he recognized as well as others. Eclipses of sun and moon were frequent during his last three years, and a black sunspot was visible for seven days."[21] A fireball raced across the sky and frightened Charlemagne's horse so that it threw him off. Earthquakes and lightning bolts indicated the sigificance of his impending death.

In the ninth century, such cosmic testimonials of sympathy or antipathy were taken at face value. Later court poets and mural painters had only allegorical intentions when they showed their heroes guided and guarded by winged, bare-bosomed females. Nevertheless, the spirit of history was considered supernatural up to modern times. Hitler still trusted a special providence set up for him.

Nowadays the spirit of history appears somewhat deflated. We have learned that small, prosaic events often have tremendous consequences for human affairs. We might call it the law of minimal causes in history. Insignificant occurrences can exert surprising leverage on the vagaries of human destiny.

One example: Napoleon lost the battle of Waterloo because his hemorrhoids acted up. English historian Colin Cross relates that on July 16, 1815, Bonaparte had victory within his reach after pushing Wellington into an untenable position. But during that night he suffered an attack of hemorrhoidal inflammation and therefore postponed his own attack against the British, giving Wellington time to regroup his forces.

Historians have usually avoided registering such earthbound bits of information. They shouldn't. A great deal of world history has depended on how well the leaders slept and digested.

Thus history has all the earmarks of the frail, vulnerable, overextended human character. It does not have that aura, that sublime configuration, which the painters of historical subjects from the sixteenth to the nineteenth centuries esteemed so highly. The beginning of Islam, for instance, seems hardly portentous: It is told that Mohammed owned a tame pigeon that used to perch on his shoulder and whisper divine advice into his ear. A cheap sleight-of-hand: He hid wheat kernels in his ear, and the hungry bird stuck its beak into Mohammed's prophetic hearing apparatus. If the Arabs had not then been convinced by this miracle to believe in the divine inspiration of their prophet, Egypt would not have become Islamic, and the Israeli-Egyptian Six-Day War would not have taken place thirteen centuries later.

Every cause must have had many previous causes: this is the point which the glorifiers of historic personalities and actions like to leave out of their considerations. On the other hand, how far should you go back when you explore antecedents? To Neanderthal man or to the first algae? Some historians, in explaining World War II, remind us that a medieval pope ordered the crusaders, who did not succeed in Palestine, to christianize the heathen Prussians instead. These knights, in a hurry to prove their valor, left the West Prussians to their Slavic customs and advanced right away to subdue more easterly tribes, who then were Germanized. Hence the Polish Corridor, Danzig, Hitler.

It seems logical. Yet what were the causes of the Christian knights' failure in the Holy Land? And the causes of these causes? Innumerable questions must be answered before we can reconstruct a causal chain. And is it worthwhile in the end?

We happen to know what formed Lenin's character: It was the execution of his elder brother by czarist oppressors. But what do we know about the inner motives of Genghis Khan, the "Emperor of all Men"? Many historians assume that they are sufficiently informed about Hitler's career. However, on the thousands of factual pages which I have read about the Führer, I could not find a clear explanation of his anti-Semitism. On the pinnacle of his success, Hitler once remarked offhandedly: "The Jews, too, once have laughed at me. Do they still laugh now?" What early experience lurked in his psyche, festering and unforgivable, to cause this remark? Did a Jewish art dealer laugh about his watercolors? Or a loan shark about his meager belongings? Or a Jewish politician about his high-flung plans? That laughter is gone, irretrievably, muted by the thunder of guns and air armadas. Therefore no history writer can presume that we have entirely understood that phenomenon, Hitler.

The effectiveness of minimal causes constitutes the decisive difference between human history and biological development. Biology operates through masses, history through individuals. In genetic progress, many mutations arise and are wasted until one "takes" and establishes a new breed; in human progress, the single and single-minded reformer is the decisive factor. Animal individuals of one species are not terribly different from each other unless they are bred for diversity, like dogs, pigeons, and goldfish. Ants are interchangeable; Saint Francis and Hitler were basically different from each other. We are justified in talking of *the* dodo being extinct, *the* rattlesnake being dangerous: There are no exceptions, which makes the singular appropriate. However, when people talk about *the* German, *the* nigger, the door is opened wide to prejudice: we project from so-called group characteristics back to what one certain individual should be like, and this is seldom conclusive.

The law of minimal causes in history gives added virulence to personal idiosyncrasies, moods, and crazes. And this makes the "accidental" appearance of one sadistic or misanthropic person among many peaceful humans so terrifyingly hazardous and influential. But this same historic law also gives a chance for efficacy to gentle, philanthropic people like Gandhi, Albert Schweitzer, and Martin Luther King.

Nobody can or wants to deny that there have been straight, directional actions toward the betterment of humanity's lot; history is full of admirable testimonies to "the good" in the human spirit, such as the writing and upholding of the American Constitution, the Red Cross, Unicef. We have the capacity and often the urge to improve life on this planet. Why do we let so many opportunities go by unused? Why do some people choose unpleasant behavior when pleasant activities would be open to them? There are many striking historical instances of helpfulness, self-sacrifice, intelligent courage, and even love of one's enemy; why are there also so frighteningly many examples of satanic lust to harm one's fellows?

Groping for a mental picture of humanity's future, it would not do to close our eyes to the shadowy side of our character. We must state unequivocally that there is simply no limit to the evil which some people can inflict on other people.

In certain situations and for certain individuals, there are no restraints when it comes to torture and murder; on the contrary, there are even inhibitions against generating less than the possible maximum of pain. It is necessary to put this capacity for limitless cruelty into the equation when we try to envisage humanity's future development: our destiny may depend upon understanding this disgusting peculiarity of our species.

Around 1500 Anno Domini, hundreds of English Protestants were burned and tortured to death every year as heretics. Upon the stake of Bishop John Hooper, green wood was piled up to prolong his agony. John Foxe has left us a picturesque account:

"He became black in his mouth, his tongue was so bloated that he could not speak any more, his lips shriveled and stuck to his gums; and he beat his breast with his hands while fat, water and blood squirted from his fingertips, until one of his arms fell off." Foxe also writes about the burning of Perrotine Massey: "Being heavy with child, she fell in the fire on her side, where the woman's belly burst. The child fell into the fire, and when it was pulled out, it was brought before the bailiff who ordered that it be laid into the flames again."

Such visually impressive descriptions are more gripping than any statistics. When we read that the Thirty Years' War reduced the population of Germany from 18 million to 6 million, we find it tragic; but the varnish of official historiography isolates the facts from our feelings. Bartolomé de Las Casas wrote a report on the extermination of 12 or 15 million Indians—some maintain that it was 20 million—by the Spaniards. Published in 1552, this powerful condemnation of the so-called Christian conquistadores excites the passions of South American and Spanish historians to this day. Have we learned something from these gruesome events? We must doubt it, considering the mass murders of Auschwitz, Hiroshima, Biafra, Bangladesh, Cambodia, and so on.

An understandable, though undesirable, reaction to these historical reports is sheer desperation concerning human nature. It would be a more useful response to see to it that such inspiring figures as Fray Bartolomé de Las Casas finally get a prominent place among the true heroes in our historical consciousness. Every student learns about conquerors like Cortez and Pizarro. Las Casas did not lack success: he was named "Protector of all the Indians" by Emperor Charles V; through indefatigable sermons, memorandums, journeys, and political maneuvers he accomplished the gradual cessation of the massacres of South America's Indians. However, this great man remains unmentioned in many school history books.

Compassion in the literal sense—suffering with somebody—is not always called for. This is true, for example, for surgeons or soldiers. Nonetheless, a surgeon welcomes every advance in anesthesiology, because a patient's pain interferes with the efficient progress of the operation. But will a general, in the same interest, look for possibilities to reduce suffering or to avoid killing? Hardly.

We are told that Napoleon's general staff, observing the burning of Moscow, actually felt pity. "The poor people", said one, "to be without a roof in this cold." Another one remarked: "A terrible sight." Napoleon, unmoved, corrected them: every destroyed enemy was, for him, a cause for rejoicing. "The smell of an enemy corpse is always sweet!" The informant adds that when he noticed the emperor's coldness of soul, his hair stood on edge.

Average human beings feel disgust when they see or read about excesses of cruelty; and undoubtedly there were entire epochs and peoples who were mainly peaceable and strove to avoid hurting others. Some societies, however, seem to have had a definite need for cruelty. Tortures and executions were accepted with equanimity as long as the reasons for subduing certain fellow humans were felt to be valid—that is to say, as long as religious, nationalistic, imperialistic, or racist motives were alive.

To present the horror as pure fact, let me select, out of innumerable similar occurrences, one instance with which we cannot identify, since both parties are equally repulsive to us. In 1959 Trujillo, the dictator of the Dominican Republic, was murdered. His supporters in the military secret intelligence service arrested his brother-in-law, General René Román Fernandez, whom they suspected of having participated in the killing. They sewed his eyelids to his eyebrows and let him lie like that for four days. Then they beat him up, poured acid over him, allowed vicious ants to crawl over him, gave him electric shocks in Trujillo's private electric chair, and finished him off with fifty-six bullets.

Well, human beings are simply horrible creatures, you say? Objectively, this is not the case. Such actions are generally called "inhuman," not typically human. The old saying "Homo hominis lupus," "Man is a wolf to his fellow man," does not apply to the majority of "normal" people on this earth. But just as erroneous is the opposite theorem proposed by Plato: "Be sure that no evil can befall a good man, neither in life nor after death." Millions of good, just, helpful, productive, irreplaceable men and women have been subjected to hunger, loneliness, disdain, torture and death.

The human conscience, in all its strength, is applied too selectively. Some mental athletes can jump over all ten commandments as if they were so many hurdles. But let's not forget the fact that humanity first had to erect these barriers!

The moral law within each person, for which Kant felt the same admiration as for the fixed stars in the sky, may not be unchanging and absolute; it has only an average efficiency, a statistical validity. But many natural phenomena and laws have nowadays been reduced to statistical probabilities. And still they are valid and true.

Sometimes, in a dreamy mood, I see legions marching across the foggy earth, blinded masses of men driven on by shouted commands, trumpets, radio signals; they fall upon each other, grey ocean waves, breaking, ebbing away. Bled-out armies sink into the humus, become fertilizer, plants cover them with green grace.

Then I see the few last ones arise, shivering in the blue dawn, they huddle together in a cave to warm each other, to procreate, to think. Has this not been our history, once before? Shreds of dreams overlap. A clan of primitive humanoids crouches in a circle. They sharpen their stone axes. One of them sits apart, tentatively he puts a stone into a leather sling. *The better weapon!* It will save us from the aggressors! Boldly he goes forth to encounter a blaring, boisterous crowd of enemies; and before he is within reach of their clubs, he shoots his missile, the leader over there falls, the others flee. Final victory! Unconditional surrender! From now on *we* will determine history, *we* will state once and for all what is just and right. Why won't the new enemies acknowledge this—those, who slink closer there in the bushes? Can't they see that the better weapon has already saved all humankind?

A catapult is pushed onto a hill, cocked, loaded, the missile whirls into the air, an eye-blistering light shows a rising cloud, giant poisonous mushrooms sprout all over the earth—the better weapon!

Again the unsurpassable better weapon.

The saddest part of our potential self-destruction through nuclear weapons is that there may be nobody around any more to appreciate the Sistine Chapel, *Hamlet,* and Beethoven's Ninth Symphony. No brain will register them as the world's most sublime works. Even if fish or cockroaches should survive the holocaust, the inestimable greatness of our works will forever remain just that—unesteemed.

The iconoclasts (before the Council of Nicaea), the Thuringian anabaptists of 1524, the rebels of the French Revolution—they all destroyed statues and paintings of saints, but at least they knew what they were doing: they did not want people to worship graven images. In a way, this was a recognition of these important, albeit hated, symbols. The Turkish lime-burners who destroyed antique Greek marble architecture and statues to make mortar for their own buildings were perhaps not consciously against art; they were only stupid.

Even within the framework of Western civilization, culture always held a precarious position. Culture must be consciously protected and cared for; it won't automatically win out over its enemies. We have to uphold our own human values with an *absolute resolve,* because to the rest of the world they are relative values at best.

A dog who lifts his leg to urinate on a classical statue of Apollo would not be "wrong" in any human sense: a statue or a fireplug are, for him, signaling devices where he can leave a message for other passing dogs. We cannot read these sociable canine signals, and they cannot read ours.

A visitor from another planet who discovered the depopulated earth would perceive a telephone directory and a volume of Shakespeare's works as one and the same: yellowed paper with black dots. All our so-called eternal values would be, at best, enigmatic curios.

We should give our grandchildren a chance to receive our signals.

When we looked at biological development, we found a marvelous directedness toward increased efficiency, complication, and beautification. In contrast, when we looked at human history, we encountered a discouraging overall aimlessness and unfeelingness that might lead to the self-destruction of both humankind and the biosphere.

How is this frightening and seemingly illogical contradiction possible?

I will admit that, out of the multitude of biological data, I favored the progressive, peaceful, and friendly ones; whereas, in presenting historical events, I selected abominations and signs of danger. Only in this way could I make the contrast impressive enough. Since I do look on the human development as on a continuation of life's career in general, it should be clear that I consider the nonsense and horror in history as temporary phenomena, as a gigantic aberration of life, as a self-denial of our true "nature."

All these wars, these religious, dynastic, economic, and other impersonal quarrels remain, in spite of their tragic consequences, only flat foreground movements that tend to obstruct our view of the essential, spiritual development of mankind. And that seems to warrant a conditional optimism.

Many compulsive action patterns that have hindered true progress are already dissolving. For instance: No world leader today declares an aim to acquire martial glory. In the olden times, a leader who did not at least once ride into battle could not get a place in the history books. This craze has passed. The writers and the makers of history have changed their tastes.

The primitive idea that a man had to prove his masculinity by putting a dozen children into the world, or by venting his frustrations in the local inn by knifing some other young man, has become out-of-date, on the village level as well as on the highest political stage. Those two proofs of manliness—namely, to be fruitful and frightful—made some sense through thousands of years insofar as they cancelled each other out, thus providing two crude kinds of amusement. They chased away the boredom of our ancestors. Today we must renounce both the overproduction of babies and of corpses, because their equilibrium is no longer attained automatically. Both pastimes have become too dangerous.

Once we admit that nature is not—repeat: not—"red in tooth and claw" and that a generally cooperative equilibrium is indeed the overriding purpose of nature, we can strive for naturally peaceful developments. In this we can be helped by integrating biology and philosophy into biosophical thinking.

We can dislocate our truly "offensive" drives and redirect our energy toward new aims. Aggressive initiative is perfectly fine if it is targeted against the foes of humankind, against sickness, hunger, and neglect—for life's sake.

4. Unstable Human Nature

"Look, I'm flying faster than you!" said the fly to the airplane while buzzing forward through its belly.

Does our endangered species merit to be preserved for a brighter future?

The highest valuation of humankind comes, perhaps, from Sophocles:

Much is powerful. But nothing
is more powerful than man.
For he roams about in the gray sea,
through wild Southern winds, through roaring waves
within his winged dwellings.
The gods' holy earth,
the pure, unconcerned one, he tills.
He throws the yoke on the long-maned horse
and on the ferocious bull.

It is a saddening thought that we could evoke such enthusiasm only in the early morning of our civilization.

Something went awry with the human character. The church father Saint Jerome could only admit dejectedly: "*Errare humanum est,*" "To err is human." Must we turn this around for a definition: To be human is to err—?

The ancient cultures sank down into rubble. Medieval man hastened to acknowledge fate's cruelty as just punishment and saddled himself with the dogma of original sin. In the Judeo-Christian world, the concept of "man" has never again attained the golden radiance it possessed for the Greeks. In modern languages the word "human" acquired a tinge of modesty and vulnerability. "He is only human," we say when some lofty dignitary has blundered. "Human frailties" are thought characteristic for the species.

Molière made his mocker Scapin exclaim: *"Il faut se laisser vaincre et avoir de l'humanité."* "To be human is to let yourself be conquered." This is the opposite of Sophocles' picture of humanity.

Rousseau believed that we were originally considerate and good, whereas Oswald Spengler decreed: "Man is a predaceous animal." Such contradictions in the definition of one and the same object are not only contrary to logic but also, in practice, full of dangers. Rousseau's precept "back to nature" is advantageous only if it does not signify "back to our predatory nature."

Schiller was inclined to count human beings among the most rapaceous animals: "Dangerous it is to awake the lion, destructive is the tiger's tooth; but the most terrible of terrors is man in his delusions."

So, which is it: Do we long for bloody fights? Do we yearn for a protective, all-enveloping technosphere? Are we products of our environment, or free spirits choosing our own aims, our own purpose?

One decisive characteristic of homo sapiens is this: he is the slowest starter among all living beings. He uses up more years in reaching adulthood than most other animals.

Our long period of immaturity also amounts to a certain retardation in sexual and political matters. Immature behavior, having proved so advantageous for the learning process, tends to linger on when maturity is required.

The slow starting ability is part of the imbalance which, in my view, is the most typical feature of the human character. As two-legged creatures, we are always in a state of unstable equilibrium. Our center of gravity is located too high above the support, and our base is much too narrow to permit us to come to rest in our usual, and most effective, upright position. Inwardly, as well as relative to the outside world, our instability commits us to forward movement. Only speedy progress can give the Occidental mind a feeling of at least temporary stability and balance.

This basic insecurity may be the subconscious reason why we strive to augment our speed. Faster transportation, speedier cooking, speed-reading, instant communication with faraway places: there is no end to this game. Of course, it is useful to save time; but is this the real motivation for our explosive acceleration? Are we not running away from deep-seated fears of an impending fall?

Be that as it may: our ever increasing mobility may still carry us on to yet-undreamed-of adventures and accomplishments.

Our directional start is not reversible, there is no turning back. Civilization—initially embodied in tools, fire, painting, counting and writing—is now part of our physiological constitution.

We cannot even drink in the direct way all animals can. They lower their heads to the water's surface; the beak, the lapping tongue, or the trunk touches the water, and the eyes can look out for enemies. If you tried to slurp from the surface, water would enter your nose and eventually you would suffocate. Bowls and flasks are not an artsy-craftsy luxury, they are indispensable: They serve to raise the water level to the mouth without wetting the face. The hand must have been the first auxiliary drinking implement when our jaws receded. But the hand was impractical for carrying water to the dwelling cave and to the first cultivated fields, and the pot became a necessity. Thus today we are a race that cannot manage a primitive activity like drinking in the original fashion.

Without knife and fire even Stone-Age people could or would not prepare their food. Furs and textiles soon became essential to those who wanted to extend their habitat into colder climates. Today only exceptionally hardy individuals can live in direct contact with raw nature, and only for limited periods. A person who can survive a wilderness experience by eating wild berries, roots, and bird eggs, seems to us *extraordinary, out of the ordinary.* The decision against any uncultured behavior style was taken irrevocably by our distant ancestors.

Once chosen, this path led on and on in one direction. Instead of adapting ourselves to our surroundings, we had the temerity of adapting our environment to ourselves. Plowed fields, highways and skyscrapers, railroads and dams, oil derricks and airports have all put our seal on the landscape; but by subordinating nature to our will, we also made ourselves dependent on the enormously complicated and sometimes frightening mechanism of civilization.

No wonder that some people gifted with a sense of fantasy occasionally tried to break out of these compulsive rites. This is what prompted Marie Antoinette's court to play shepherds among straw-thatched, artifically primitive huts right in the park of Versailles. And a similar revulsion against the constraints of mechanized mores generated the lifestyle of the hippie communes.

The earliest human artifact we have is a stone chopper of Pekin Man. What remains of our distant ancestors are mainly their weapons: hand-axes, arrowheads, knives. This has given rise to the popular picture of a rough, bloodstained meat-eater, which I think is a faulty extrapolation. Perhaps Abel's competition with Cain was grounded on fact! Early man's vegetarian meals have left hardly any traces, whereas the bones on which he and she chewed have been found. Perhaps some of these tribes had a rather peaceful mentality.

The first habit-forming tool must certainly have been a wooden stick; but, because wood rots, we don't discover these sticks on prehistoric campsites. Had primitive people not known exactly how to use the staff for multiple tasks, they could not have combined it with spear tips, axes, and arrowheads. And some societies still use the planter's stick for burying seeds.

Why did early man need a stick? The reason was not his aggressive character, but a biological peculiarity. *Homo erectus,* upright man, never quite overcame the awkwardness that had to be taken into the bargain when the four-handed mode of life was abandoned. Because our bodies have adapted to the erect stance, stoop labor is considered degrading.

Actually, very few animals that developed an imbalanced physique still functioned and survived successfully. All long-legged vertebrates possess either a correspondingly long neck—such as the ostrich, stork, and giraffe; or a long, strong tail—such as the iguanodon, kangaroo, and jumping desert mouse—as a third, supporting "leg"; or they possess elongated arms, as do the anthropoid apes. There seems to be a morphological law demanding that animal bodies tend toward a compositional balance of their main parts. Only man revolted against this law, preferring imbalance. When he stood up on two legs and brought his spine into a habitually vertical position, he could no longer use his arms to accomplish tasks connected with the soil. Instead of succumbing to this "shortcoming" in a nice, Darwinian way, he adopted the wooden stick for use as a hoe, as a support in old age or infirmity, as a weapon, as the shepherd's crook, and finally as a symbol of superior power still in use today with bishops, field marshals, orchestra conductors, and policemen. Had he not "stumbled" on these uses of the staff to extend the reach of his upper body, it is likely that selective pressure would have forced him, in the course of many generations, to develop elongated, spidery arms.

Extension of the all-too-short arm: Here we have the formula for the incessantly widening function of the machine. The prolongation of man's severely limited reach to conduct his volitional impulses toward faraway objects was too seductive a possibility and, once discovered, an unlimited one.

The invention of the weapon had an unfavorable secondary consequence: killing became more impersonal. During the course of 400 million years, killing had taken place through bodily contact, often in forms of fair combat. To kill and to eat were usually phases of one psychophysical action. The entire personality of the killer was thrown into the act. A certain risk was involved in strangling, biting, or tearing up the victim, whereas shooting one's prey with an inanimate object can be a one-sided affair. But since we stood naked and without large teeth and claws in the midst of the rather inhospitable surroundings of the Ice Age, we chose this solution to minimize danger. Only close combat or tilting were still oriented toward personal valor in bodily proximity; dueling with sword or rapier, jousting, *jiu jitsu* were prearranged to give the adversary an equal chance, and thus they inevitably developed into formalized sports. Dropping a bomb, on the other hand, is obviously not restricted by any knightly ideas. The improvement of weapons led necessarily to denatured combat, where it is no longer necessary to look at the enemy—indeed, it is better for modern soldiers not even to imagine what their victims might be like, otherwise the overwhelming potential of misery might give them pause. Thus people are converted as by magic into faceless military targets.

This, then, is the great imbalance that *Homo erectus* introduced into the biosphere. The lack of equilibrium in his bodily form (with the all-too-short arm and the narrow base of his feet) found its projection into our own delicate balance with nature.

When men and women acquired and refined tools, they stepped out of the sphere of creatures led mainly by their instincts: The use of tools presupposes more insight into their various possible functions than the use of limbs. Limbs have just one natural way of working—their hinges turn only in certain directions, and they are permanently connected to the body. You cannot shed a limb simply by using it in an inappropriate way. But utensils must be held firmly at one end, while the other end has to be connected to its field of operation. This means that you must first pay attention to the tool itself, not only to its purpose; and divided attention demands thinking. A tool forms a threefold bridge from the brain through a limb to the intended object, and this complicated connection has to be renewed and maintained during use. Mastery of the tool is reached when this connection becomes quasi-organic, and this early automation offers tremendous practical advantages.

With that step, the function of learning enters irrevocably into our way of living. Intelligence becomes as important as any instinct. The role of parents and older peers in a group is magnified: as teachers, they become indispensable.

Learning seems practically impossible without a close bond between parents and offspring; and in this the warm-blooded animals have a definite advantage. True, many cold-blooded creatures manage to care for their brood, some in elaborate ways. Such varied animals as the scorpion and the South American honeycomb toad have hit on the same solution to assemble and protect their young ones: They carry them around on their backs. The male stickleback goes to the extreme of carefully sucking his infants into his mouth to keep them out of harm's way. But most cold-blooded animals could not care less whether their brood develops or perishes. These species usually produce such overwhelming quantities of eggs and babies that their statistical chance for survival is high even without parental care. But the function of the parental bond augments radically as soon as learning becomes important. Then the parents have to invest much time and energy in their kindergarten.

It is not so much the process of learning but of teaching that makes all the difference.

Learning occurs even on the primitive rungs of evolutionary development. Worms have been trained to avoid certain corners of a maze by regularly receiving electric shocks at these spots. But learning with understanding occurs first in warm-blooded animals because their young ones depend on intimate contact with their parents: They must be kept warm until their feathers or fur have developed (and until their mass has grown big enough, proportionate to their surface, to retain sufficient body heat; small bodies lose heat faster). This closeness, which is demanded physiologically, is conducive to teaching situations; imitation leads to learning, to admiration of parents, to the ambition to do as well as other members of the group, and finally to a unified, interdependent, structured civilization.

Behavioral scientists do not yet agree as to how much of the activities of flying, hunting, enemy recognition, and flight reaction comes with inherited instincts and how much is genuine, individual learning. A baby hare that is to be weaned from its mother's milk takes the first leaves of grass from the mother's lips; it does not pick them directly from the meadow. Ever since I first observed such charming scenes in my youth, I have been inclined to believe in an almost intelligent exchange of teaching and learning among many warm-blooded creatures.

A certain retrogression is typical for the human species: "Playing dumb" initiates our smartness and skill. The newborn homo sapiens cannot cling to its mother's body, a feat any monkey baby is capable of. It cannot walk like a new foal; it cannot even crawl, as blind dog puppies do; it cannot do a thing—except attract the general attention by ear-shattering cries, which makes sense only among helpful adults, not among enemies. Its cuteness, its ability to touch your heart, is not its own merit. A human baby is more helpless than most other young placental mammals, except perhaps the two-inch-long baby of the Giant Panda.

However, this initial stupidity, this step backwards, makes the flying start possible. Thus the baby of *genus humanum* learns how to learn.

It would be nice if pupils could slice up and ingest the brain of a dying professor, thus acquiring his expertise. This would make for a beautiful ceremony. But it does not work that way.

Learning has many advantages and one single disadvantage.

Its drawback is that its results are not inheritable. The knowledge that has entered the brain of the wisest savant dies with that brain; no stored imprints can ever modify the genes. Studying has to begin anew with each individual. No memory contents are passed on to any embryo through sperm cells or ova. Year after year, we must spend huge sums for schooling, and learned persons must spend much of their valuable time transmitting their own results in writing or orally to younger pupils and colleagues. Only from the outside, entering through the channels of their senses, can knowledge be transmitted into new brains. Every child must absorb the knowledge he or she needs either through imitation or through the hard, sometimes painful, sometimes joyously satisfying act of studying.

In spite of these difficulties, acquired knowledge in a well-organized society does not get lost; instruction connects the generations almost automatically. Only when a certain culture becomes shaky, when traditional learning no longer pays, when an uninstructed person can acquire much power—then information and skills are forgotten and erased. History knows frequent periods when ignorants and iconoclasts conquered entire civilizations.

This isolation in time is the disadvantage of learning. What, seen without value judgment, are its advantages?

Every human organism possesses both inherited and acquired characteristics. The number of inherited qualities is strictly limited. By contrast, the number of acquired qualities is, in principle, unlimited. They offer a much larger potential for growth and diversification. Once the collecting and integration of acquired properties and knowledge have started, their progress can lead into the highest augmentation—into outer space, for instance. Or into a terrestrial organization dedicated to the elimination of war and want. Learning has no upward limit.

The potentially immense importance of even a single human life is due to the feedback function of imitation and example. Within the frame of reference of one character the inherited properties tend toward the status quo, they show an amazing inertia or conservatism; acquired characteristics, on the other hand, provoke dynamic behavior. This means that the higher development of life must necessarily favor the individual. The higher we ascend on life's family tree, the more it branches out, and individual differences are favored; and as the crowning achievement we find personal initiative. This, in turn, means that the malleable single being can advance its race better than the race itself, which is hampered by its built-in inertia. If we had to wait for the tedious process of natural selection to produce our improvements, no progress would be recognizable for many generations. As a teacher or model, one single personality can reshape entire populations and cultures. Here again the "law of minimal causes" is at work.

Learning is the instrument for our accelerated adaptation to the technosphere whose innovations, though caused by us, now form an integral part of the natural world. Learning must be more than the collecting and absorbing of raw data, it must change our entire character makeup. In this manner, through an increasing refinement of the type homo sapiens, it continues the progress that governed the animal kingdom for more than 500 million years, producing ever more complicated, efficient, mobile, clever, and also beautiful types.

Our acquired properties have become a precarious but indispensable dowry. their multiplicity—the number and variation of acquired actions and reactions—is unlimited and illimitable. This makes learning such a flexible instrument that it justifies limitless hopes.

The civilizing process is basically not more unnatural than the preceding development by "natural" selection. Up to the appearance of the Hominidae, evolution is considered autonomous; did it then suddenly become artificial? Is an intellectual perhaps not governed by hunger and love? Nature and culture are not contrasting phenomena, but partial stretches of one directional development.

A short résumé may be in order. *Homo erectus,* separated from the soil by an upright stance and yet handicapped by a short reach, was forced to produce tools in order to utilize that soil—and tools required civilized thought processes. After we had tools, there was no selective pressure to elongate the forelimbs. The idea of the useful implement originated physiologically—that is, naturally. The rising complication of our technicized way of life, which often makes us sigh for simpler circumstances, is still only a continuation of nature's development: That also started with primitive, simple forms and, through the ages, exaggerated its multiplicity. "Back to nature"? We are right inside nature: many plants, animals, and their molecules, too, became ever more complex.

These tendencies, brought into harmony, open up an almost limitless richness of life.

Here is my (slightly cut-rate) story of man's creation.

When the Creator, on the sixth day, got around to making Adam, his creative activities had tired him. He would have done better to rest on the sixth day and to invent homo sapiens on Monday morning, when his mind was fresh. For reasons unknown, he was in a hurry; perhaps he feared that his inspiration might run out. All those ideas that really belonged to the first five creative days buzzed around in his overworked imagination. Thus he mixed all sorts of incoherent features into poor Adam: a chunk of beastliness; some angels' matter, paradisiacal contentment and chaotic yearnings; oceanic, limitless hope; and the dull limitations of a clod of earth. Crapulous waste and cosmic radiance.

"Humanity must perforce prey on itself, like monsters of the deep." Is the Duke of Albany, in Shakespeare's "King Lear", right? Are we beasts of prey, as Spengler and many minor fascist writers maintained? The great psychologist William James wrote: "Seen biologically, man is the most terrible of all predatory animals." Is this correct?

Many a civilized citizen harbors the secret wish to be a free-roaming animal, overpowering others with a minimum of effort and a maximum of grace. We name our automobiles "Cougar" or "Jaguar" even though we use them mostly on congested, smoggy streets. The human male is flattered when a woman calls him "tiger"; he in turn hangs animal skins around her shoulders. But I like the observation of an elderly gentleman whose wife was looking longingly into a furrier's shop window: "If God had meant you to wear a mink coat, he would have created you as a mink."

As a matter of fact, it is our good fortune that we are not predators. Anatomically, homo sapiens is an omnivore, just like our dear pig. Human teeth can grind up plants, and they can also cut small pieces from a chunk of meat. No predator could go about his business with our soft, thin claws. Human mentality is constituted for circumspection, not for the sudden, overwhelming expense of all latent energy. Beasts of prey, from the spider to the lion, must be equipped for one single, decisive pounce, for life as a gambling operation. Human beings, though agile and relatively strong, reach their important aims through perseverance; our typical endeavor is to attack one purpose from several possible angles.

Admittedly, the proud, reticent carnivores like eagle and panther offer a nobler impression than the always busy pigs and monkeys. In spite of this aesthetic preference, we should not establish the hunter as our ideal. Napoleon replaced the Gallic cock with the

Roman eagle as the national emblem of France: He opined that chanticleer on the dung heap was not dignified enough to represent a great nation. Napoleon depopulated France and wasted Europe's riches. His works have evaporated, but the French rooster still remains scratching through the dung, a friendly symbol of ecocirculation—and not without his own measure of dignity.

An island or even a continent that would be populated by peaceful herbivores exclusively could support its fauna and stay fertile through innumerable generations. By contrast, if we imagine a region teeming only with carnivores, it would obviously become depopulated after two or three generations, and the killers would be reduced to devouring each other.

Where the big cats have been eliminated, deer and gazelles at first become too numerous and shrubs so denuded that they die; but soon hunger diminishes the number of herbivores again, whereupon the meadows and bushes recover. Without the meateaters, a new bioeconomic balance emerges, and the result is by no means catastrophic. Yet without plant-eaters, the solar energy that collects in the flora could not be transferred to animals at all, and consequently the entire fauna would disappear.

If there were no domestic cats, there would be more "harmful" mice; but there would also be more "useful" songbirds. On the environmental ledger, plus and minus tend to equalize each other.

Of course, this is not an argument against keeping cats, nor against protecting insect-eating birds. But we don't have to glorify the utility of the killers. Nothing is amiss if living flesh rounds out its natural existence and then sinks back into the topsoil.

It would be presumptuous to argue against the existence of the genuine predatory animals: they enjoy their own existence, even though they inflict fright and pain on other beings. However—and this is the important point—nature does not need a pseudo-predator who eradicates other species and indulges his bloodthirstiness in periodic wars. Nietzsche's famed "blond beast" is simply not needed.

If the human condition is not that of a predator, what, then, is it? What is the opposite of robbery? Exchange, obviously. Production and commerce. Just payment, mutual aid, world traffic, free barter of goods and ideas. An open world in which frontiers become, at the most, symbolic of historical configurations, and in which distances and differences tend to melt. Does this sound too prosaic? Then we should consider that in such a world Kant's categorical imperative has some chance for effectiveness: "Act only in such a way that the maxim of your action could become a universal law." No predatory animal could wish that its prey should reciprocate. No carnivore could, according to his constitution, ever conceive the Golden Rule.

Much enjoyment that comes easily to peaceful denizens of the earth is lost to carnivores. Love itself is often falsified through an aggressive character. A male spider, small and timid, must approach his nasty female cautiously with a wrapped-up fly as a mollifying gift in order not to be eaten by her before copulation— a fate from which he won't escape after having fulfilled his marital duty. The praying mantis goes even further: She chews up the head and chest of her mate while his posterior parts accomplish their biological task. This cannot be very satisfying.

As early as 1902, Peter Kropotkin tried to show that mutual aid in nature is more important than combat. Yet even that gentle soul was sure that "the vast majority of animals feed on other animals which belong to different zooligical categories."[22] Did no one see that carnivores comprise only a small minority among animals? Did no one bother to count?

Our school biology books taught us to discriminate between harmful and useful animals. Later on we usually found that things are more complicated, that "use" for one is "harm" for another. Still, both naturalists and laypeople agree that little birds are needed for insect control, that small four-footed carnivores are indispensable to keep a check on rodents. Cats, weasels, finches, spiders are useful; mice, aphids, caterpillars are noxious. Yet even this "pro-predator argument" can just as well be turned around.

The rodents were forced, through selection pressure, to become overly fertile in the first place. If there were no weasels, foxes, and cats, rats would be quite happy with only two babies a year, and zero population growth would triumph in mousedom. Caterpillars have to be generated in such overwhelming numbers precisely because they have so many enemies. It is like a seesaw: more predators on one side require more plant eaters on the other side. If there were no insect-eating birds, the insects that lay only a few eggs would get their share of the pie exactly as the more fertile ones, and thus would not die out. The availability of green food would regulate the numbers of these insects very efficiently, and the danger of periodic epidemics by swarms of tree-moths and grasshoppers would not exist: These species simply would never reproduce in such terrifying numbers, they would not have developed the capacity for fast, overwhelmingly numerous breeding. This fecundity brings with it the danger that, if even one controlling factor happens to be missing one year, things immediately get out of hand and a flood of unwanted offspring competes for the available food and makes all other creatures of the region miserable.

Control generates the uncontrolled potential in the first place; therefore we might just as well include the cats and swallows among the "harmful" beasts! But the whole argument is awry, of course. In nature there is no harm nor use as such, there is only the web of life; and we must simply see to it that this web serves us as a garment and not as a shroud.

This is the crucial point where Darwin, in my opinion, created a new myth. "Every single organic being," he wrote, "may be said to be striving to the utmost to increase in numbers; . . . each lives by a struggle at some period of its life; heavy destruction inevitably falls either on the young or old during each generation or at recurrent intervals. Lighten any check, mitigate the destruction ever so little, and the number of their species will almost instantaneously increase to any amount."

This is far too dogmatic.

As I stated earlier, animals with few or no natural enemies—such as whale, bear, chimpanzee, kangaroo, vulture—tend to have few babies. What is the explanation for this natural birth control? It might be a Darwinian connection: Their unmolested circumstances don't select for the overly fertile individuals among these races. Thus there is no danger of population explosion in these species—even, and this is significant, without enemies. Unfortunately, humans in their primitive stages had to resort to defense through numbers; and therefore, when natural enemies—from tigers to tubercle bacilli—were eliminated, our reserve faculty of producing large numbers got out of hand.

I love cats, even though I dislike the sight of gentle pussy playing around with a hapless mouse for twenty minutes before giving it the *coup de grâce*. I admire hawks and wolves, tigers and snakes, and I wish with all my heart that they would be preserved in significant numbers: They are part of the world we love. However, I hate the reverse sentimentality that admires the robber baron's way of life, as exemplified by heraldic eagle and lion.

I'm against the "scientific" prejudice that the fauna of a predator-free island is somehow inferior. True, the dodo and the kiwi birds lost their faculty of flight because they were never chased by enemies; but did this make their lives less rounded, less gratifying to themselves? Were the sailors who landed on Mauritius in the seventeenth century and laughingly clubbed the trusting dodos to death the more admirable creatures because they were "the fittest"?

Where in nature's realm does cruelty occur?

Not, of course, in the most primitive forms. The originally inanimate, rocky crust of our planet was slowly decomposed by weather, bacteria, algae, lichens. Once the basic step of building life from minerals is accomplished, life feeds on organic matter—but usually on organisms that have already died. Plants earn an honest living by fixing solar energy, by reconstituting minerals and humus. Only the higher forms exploit the energy and matter accumulated by the more primitive organisms, usually without regard to whether or not they are still alive. But even this cannot yet be called cruelty: The exploiters take care not to "kill the goose that lays the golden egg." Grazing animals are never root-eaters.

Seed-eaters don't digest all the seeds, but distribute some of them again in their excrements. Active cruelty occurs only toward the top of the evolutionary ladder, as a tool of the hunter. When the edible animals develop ruses, inventiveness, agility, and enough speed to escape, their persecutors find it desirable to intimidate the intended victims by hypnotic and cruel attitudes: The hunter wants to appear in the guise of inescapable fate. In this context it suddenly pays to play around with a wounded captive for a while, demonstrating to his family how effortlessly the kill can be accomplished: The uselessness of defense is brought home. Such behavior patterns of some winged and four-footed meat-eaters resemble what, in human relations, would be called intimidation, bullying, revenge; and these highly developed psychological structures have continued right on into our civilization, becoming more and more dangerous and vicious.

Yet as omnivores, which is our true nature, we must rely on the harmony of widely divergent forces within the entire biosphere—more so than any specialized animal. For us the war of all against all (which Thomas Hobbes stipulated for nature) would only mean war against our own best interests.

It is an extremely hopeful sign of the times that some of the most diverse people—biologists, political leaders, journalists, students—have developed a revulsion against the maltreatment of our earth. Within a few years the attitude of humanity toward fouling its nest has completely changed. If this endeavor survives the period of sloganizing and politicking, it will justify our trust in the human capacity for survival.

We know—and we don't mind—that the cat who lives within our circle of intimacy, who wants to be petted and flatters us with love signals, has a different world view from our own. Its instinctive actions are triggered by different features of the environment. If we tried to look at the world from inside a cat's head, a mousehole or a bird's-nest would appear more attractive than an apple or a rose. The perceptual world of a bee must be unimaginably different from anything we experience. All we want from our domestic animals is that their behavior be reasonably predictable. We consider it immaterial whether the animal itself judges in accord with our yardsticks. It suffices to agree on a time schedule that regulates our *modus vivendi* with dog, horse, cow, and hen. We wish to transmit our own sense of propriety and cleanliness to our dog, but not to our cow. We don't want to convince an animal of the correctness of our *Weltanschauung*.

But just let another human being disagree with some of our basic tenets! Right away prisons and burning piles are put into use for reeducation! Homosexuals who harmed no one were persecuted, atheists annihilated, enclaves of foreign nationalities eradicated—all in the service of ideas which were found to be erroneous after a few decades and which, in any case, were not worth these blood sacrifices.

Have we become more tolerant? In principle, certainly. We tolerate the "hereditary enemy" of years past. But we don't seem able to include the current adversary in this theoretical tolerance. The small step from selective humaneness to the prohibition of killing any human being on purpose under any circumstances— this small step seems still beyond our reach.

Human beings are more multifarious than any other species because they live in an open world, spreading all over the globe and through every climate; because they have tried and discarded many occupations and habits; because they have undertaken great tribal wanderings, conquests, slaving expeditions, and liberations that mixed together divergent types. Multifarious man had to maximize the natural tendency toward symbiosis because he eventually had to do justice to widely differentiated "foreigners" without designating them forever as subhumans. Thus "man," as image, includes some who are busy as ants, meek as lambs, hedonistic as butterflies, grouchy as bears, slippery as eels: The whole animal kingdom of fable is subsumed under the concept of "man." And yet we have to live and work together in much closer proximity than the real ant, bear, and butterfly: We have to cooperate consciously to survive.

Imbalanced man emerged when, half a million years ago, he left the protection of the forest—perhaps consequent to climatic changes, perhaps just yielding to the lust for adventure. On the open plains we had to behave more aggressively than our earlier, arboreal ancestors who, when hungry, only had to stretch out a hand in order to pluck a fruit, some juicy greenery, or insects. Now we had to become hunters and warriors without, at the same time, giving up our vegetable meals and some other peaceful pursuits. However, our body construction was not modified in accordance with our new jobs: and that is a great rarity among naturally developing species who metamorphose when confronted with new tasks. We dispensed with the selective breeding that might have given us the hunter's fangs, claws, and protective leather; our invention of weapons, tools, clothing, and fire took away the selective pressure that would have modified our species in the direction of predacious characteristics. Our bodily makeup remained that of an omnivore, but our psychological constitution had to develop traits of the hunting carnivore, at least temporarily. This was unbalancing for our psyche, it required frequent high tension and almost daily behavioral switches.

In recent times, the situation has changed again. We have succeeded in fulfilling the tasks of the open plain. It would be superfluous, even ridiculous, for us to hunt "our" cows and chickens. The big predacious animals are no longer a menace. Our bloodthirstiness—which we had to develop simply as a hunting tool—became purposeless and concentrated on intrahuman quarrels. A dangerous constellation indeed!

Now we find it a blessing that our physique has not undergone the metamorphosis into that of a predator. Thus we can return to the more joyful, modest, playful constitution which our relatives, the apes, never abandoned. We can save the evolutionary detour of atrophying dangerous claws and fangs. We only have to put down the temporary weapons of the pseudopredator.

Displacing the carnivores in the outside world was only the first step toward displacing the predacious animal in ourselves.

The most dangerous imbalance exists between our physically confined body and our immeasurable, illimitable spirit.

The human spirit has augmented its power so much that it is now more powerful than all the formerly feared and venerated spirits put together. Even in Goethe's time resignation seemed still indicated: "Alas! the spiritual wings will not easily be supplemented by any bodily wings." Faust had to sell his soul to the devil before he could use Mephisto's magic cape as a flying machine.

Isn't there a slight whiff of sulphur still clinging to "the spirit"? Unhestitatingly, we call "devilish" such accomplishments of scientific thinking as the neutron bomb. We have taken over all those faculties that were formerly ascribed to magicians and witches. Enrico Caruso, dead since 1921, sings for us: The turning of a knob is the magic rite that beckons him from his grave for our entertainment. We chat with relatives and business acquaintances who live on different continents. Strange characters materialize in a box in our living room; when these figures displease us, we make them disappear again. Very convenient, but a little eerie. Everything that the old spirits were supposed to do, the human spirit has recently accomplished. Every day has now twenty-four ghosting hours.

Even science fiction may run out of themes that are "too fantastic." From the moon to the galaxies would still be a giant step, but the human spirit has already arranged for its feasability: Einstein has ordered time itself to pass more slowly in fast-moving bodies, allowing the cosmic travelers to age more slowly than they would have on earth. Everything seems to be in good order!

Nevertheless, we cannot feel quite at ease with these supposedly rational goings-on. We must doubt whether the power of the human spirit is indeed spiritual power.

The people who calculated and executed nuclear fission and fusion are not as strong as an atom bomb; the discrepancy in strength between cause and consequence has become quite horrifying. Psychologists maintain that fantasies of omnipotence are characteristic for the infantile and the primitive psyche; but these wish-dreams of tremendous power also seem to guide the thoughts of some modern leaders, and their fantasies can now be put into practice even though they still cling to the old infantile motives.

What makes the human spirit so measureless?

The brain works like an animated film. Drawn meticulously, picture by tiny picture, a cartoon can show anything with believability. The artist can, with exactly the same expenditure of force, unfold a blossom or erect a skyscraper.

What is brain power? We don't know. The largest brain ever measured belonged to an idiot; the second largest to the writer Turgenev. Were the electrical, chemical, or yet-unknown physical properties of Lenin's earth-shaking thinking apparatus stronger than those of a fisherman, a savant, or a hooligan? Lenin's brain, after his death, was cut up into microscopically thin slices; nothing special was discovered. The food intake—the direct source of energy—is the same for a genius and a dimwit.

Thought, as an agent, is different from anything else in the natural world. Most of the restrictive natural laws are invalid for the spirit. The preservation of mass and energy is inoperative, we can imagine an apple as easily as a pyramid, both can emerge and disappear at the whim of their thinker. Thought is faster than any other motion; within a second it can rush from an atom in the laboratory to a galaxy at the limit of our known universe; it can conquer distances for which a light ray would need millions of years. Electromagnetic waves have a speed of 300,000 kilometers per second; this is the maximum velocity of all known rays, a fundamental constant of the cosmos. Only thought is not subject to that speed limit.

The explanation for this uncanny singularity is almost too simple: The voyage of one thought is not a movement of identical particles or waves through space. Nevertheless, the human spirit has the faculty of modifying things after its own image, and this makes it a quite exceptional phenomenon. We don't know where, and indeed whether, human thought has any worldly limitations.

Some other motions a physicist would not acknowledge as genuine are ocean waves (which travel for long distances and still don't transport water particles with them) and the beam of a light-house. Seen on a hazy night, the signal from a lighthouse, sweeping across the horizon, appears menacingly fast; yet nothing is really turning out there over the sea, the only circular motion takes place in the apparatus of the lighthouse itself. Nonetheless, two observers on a distant planet who would be able to measure the speed of our lighthouse beam would find that it sweeps them by at a speed greater than the speed of light.

By the way, these phantom movements (human thoughts, ocean waves, lighthouse signals) can become genuine movements if they activate relays that, in their turn, switch on servomotors or the like. A ray whose source is moved on earth could trip photoelectric cells on several heavenly bodies, thus activating a genuine sequence with greater speed than light. Are these fantasies without practical value? They could, some day, be of importance for an intergalactic communications network; and they prove, theoretically, that the phantom speed of human thought can be converted into physical reality.

The "ghostly" power of the human spirit corresponds exactly to the tricks of projection. A film of a game of billiards presents several spheres that move according to the physical laws of solid bodies: They hit and repel each other at angles determined by the shape and weight of the ivory. Yet there is no solidity whatsoever in the flickering image of the silver screen, no weight, no inertia: just light and shadow. The reproduction does not obey the laws of the projected light rays, but the mechanical laws of the photographed objects.

Schiller stated: "Thoughts dwell lightly together, but things in space push each other rudely." Still, a physicist thinking about rolling billiard balls will picture them mentally as behaving according to their observed laws, even though they don't consist of ivory, but only of tiny impulses in his or her ganglia.

What would happen if Mickey Mouse suddenly stepped out of his frame, interfered in our human surroundings, erected absurd skyscrapers, and played childish games in airplanes? But this is exactly what the human intellect is doing! It transforms the wildest ideas into actuality. Should we not be scared, then, of inept sorcerer's apprentices?

The human intellect has only imaginary strength and therefore does not function reliably. The instinctual force of a bull or a lion causes these animals to react and behave as pillars of strength, even when circumstances would favor yielding, reticence, or shyness. That impressive unity of character may have its disadvantages. But the extreme instability of the human spirit is more dangerous because it leads into contradictions, detours, and blind alleys.

Our brain is not an instrument designed for acquiring pure knowledge; it is a vital organ, specifically developed for the life of a two-legged mammal, omnivore, cave-dweller, runner, or member of a flock with centrifugal tendencies. It is strangely incongruent with our actual surroundings established by our own technology. All our strivings, even when they are directed toward objective science, social improvement, artistic creation, are tinted by our nonintellectual heritage. An aim in thought is translated into action with greater ease, speed, and satisfaction if it corresponds to this primitivistic heritage. Readily, we call those individuals "great" who were successful as warriors and hunters, bellwethers, medicine men and magicians, collectors of bounty and territory; to our instincts they are not great because they may have served our complicated culture but because they fulfill our most antiquated ideas of power and success.

The drive toward self-preservation, innate even to the worm, causes a further imbalance in ourselves and in our world view. This wish for life's continuation is so strong that it superseded the will to knowledge through thousands of years. The will to self-preservation overshoots its mark—it makes us want an immortal soul, a timeless paradise, soul-transmigration, eternal justice, and an eternal meaning to life.

Such wish-dreams often cause disagreements among adherents of different beliefs, and the resulting quarrels are real enough. Since these beliefs cannot be verified experimentally, they differ so widely from one region and epoch to the next that they cannot be harmonized with each other. And since they are overcharged with sentiments and affects, people sometimes split each others' skulls to prove that their particular idea of the soul is the correct one.

The will to self-preservation came earlier than the intellect and, therefore, seems closer to the center of our being. Just as a worm wriggles to avoid the pecking beak of a blackbird, a man in panic shakes all over: Originally, this shaking was meant to make an aggressor "see double" and to confuse his aim. The elementary drive to preserve one's life does not necessarily use intelligent means.

We have to admit that an unconditional drive toward knowledge is not essential to life. A person with a faulty liver dies; a person with a faulty philosophy can have a long and happy career. A man with a leaking heart valve suffers; a man with a short circuit in his thought system usually feels very well.

This reminds us forcefully that our original position on this planet was not that of cool, detached cognizants but of sweating, grubbing creatures who had to make their way despite great dangers and difficulties. That is one reason why many average people resent skeptics, why the aloof intellectual is not considered a "regular fellow."

Only recently, since the dawn of the atomic age, has the practical value of theoretical knowledge been generally accepted. Now we are bound to bring our instinctive heritage into balance with our rationality: We have to ration our wish-dreams.

Self-confidence is required for practical success; self-doubt, which prevents action, is biologically disadvantageous.

On these grounds normal human beings rarely permit themselves to doubt that their own view of the world is perfect. And yet our sensual knowledge of our surroundings is as incomplete as that of any animal. Each of our senses is severely specialized and can receive only a small fraction of the outside signals.

Some insects can see ultraviolet but not red. We don't expect them to know that their visual field might be faulty, and we don't expect humans to miss the color qualities of ultraviolet and infrared, which are nonexistent for our visual nerves. One-third of all the blossoms in a meadow are colored ultraviolet; every bee sees that. Are we perturbed by the fact that we are color blind to this segment of the spectrum? There are blind newts living in subterranean caves who find their way very well in the dark waters, who procreate and reach a considerable age, no doubt without feeling any deprivation.

Humans and beasts alike, in their primitive state, trust their senses. We usually act as if we were in possession of all relevant facts. The stronger one's personality, the less one is disturbed by doubts in one's fundamental rightness. A king, a priest, a warrior, an artist do not care whether their world is shot through with fantasies—as long as their activities bring them closer to their desired goals.

Children ask; adults trust their collected experiences. Only when we fail in our practical endeavors will we reexamine our assumptions: Failure is the criterium of unreality. When the mental model does not correspond to the hard facts, unpredictable developments occur. We then make a few intellectual adjustments that save our illusions. Success is never a binding proof that all pertinent mental images and all conceptions were correct; and therefore failure is not acknowledged to be a proof of incorrect thinking. We try to proceed in living without being in possession of absolute truth, and usually we manage to muddle through.

Columbus, setting sail for an impossible journey to India, can yet reach a worthwhile goal. His success proves to his own mind that his preprogrammed image of the globe was correct. Productive errors are amazingly frequent throughout history. The sober experience of latecomers usually corrects these misjudgments.

We have no sense organs to receive X-rays, ultrasound, magnetic waves. Does this deficiency knock holes in our world picture? No; for we know anyway how imperfect our sense reception is. We cannot perceive the back side of opaque objects: The back is simply missing. If an object is close at hand, we can touch its rear and get a supplementary tactile picture of its three-dimensional gestalt. But the back side of a mountain remains enigmatic until we cross that mountain. Are we perturbed by the fact that we see only that half of all objects which faces us? At times we are; and this discomfort forces us to send TV cameras around heavenly bodies. But usually we content ourselves with the thought that one of these days we might look across our backyard wall to find out what's on the other side; and we let it go at that.

Truth, the whole truth, is not a necessary precondition for our daily lives. And this shortcoming is fraught with certain dangers. It furnishes motives and temptations to all kinds of propagandists and ideologues to peddle their risky prescriptions. It favors extremists and endangers our fragile balance of human concerns.

The phototropic moth who finds it desirable to fly into the flame of a candle becomes the victim of a faulty world view, and there is no salvation from that fate. Perhaps it is our luck that some illusions destroy life: This gives a survival edge to people with knowledge and with wisdom.

A blind man spent a pleasant evening at a friend's house. When saying goodbye he insisted on going home alone, but he asked to borrow a lantern. "What for?" inquired his friend. "The lantern won't help you to see your way."

The blind man explained: "I need the lantern so that other people see me coming and avoid my path."

So he went, waving his lantern. Another pedestrian bumped into him. The blind one scolded him: "Can't you pay attention? Don't you see my lantern?"

"I'm sorry, no," said the other man politely. "I happen to be blind."

From childhood on, homo sapiens must consciously strive for balance. The toddler has to learn to keep the center of gravity directly above two relatively small feet, and the required reflex movements never become wholly automatic. Being human remains an act of tightrope walking.

Since we are obliged to handle tools whose reach, weight, and effectiveness keep expanding, this equilibrium is always put into question. Our individual ageing as well as the maturing of our civilization requires constant learning.

The greatest danger lies in the fact that our spirit itself can be transformed into a tool. Its immense leverage exposes us to an augmented imbalance. The old common sense cannot comprehend subatomic and galactic worlds; the computer is more important in these fields than sentiment.

Having been extremely successful with the tool as such, we do not sufficiently resist the transmutation of our reason—which, after all, *is in us*—into a kind of inanimate lever. Our imbalance, considering our small biological and philosophical base, becomes more and more menacing as this lever becomes ever more extended.

As one result of this lopsidedness, keeping peace is now more difficult than waging war. Our technology has mastered the art of absolute destruction: somebody could push a few buttons, and our biosphere would be largely destroyed. But the same technological know-how seems strained to its utmost capacity to prevent this from happening accidentally or rashly. The apparatus to hinder fools or fate from setting off the nuclear holocaust is more complicated and less reliable than the mechanism to start the destruction.

In order to restore the balance, we must give more weight to the truly human qualities. To stay within our simile: the dangerously extended upward lever has to be counterbalanced by depth. The deepest resources of the human soul have to be revaluated.

It is asking too much of our—otherwise admirable—reason to define this depth; this is not its province. People with some religious faith have an easier time of it: they can fall back on the descriptions of the soul and prescriptions for its tasks as expounded in their sacred scriptures. An atheist must reach his own conclusions, even if he seeks guidance from the great philosophers and, to a limited extent, from religious thinkers.

There are hours when we are certain that we *have* the sense of existence, that we partake of life's meaning. But these are not those times when our thinking is at its clearest. As to my own experience, in my younger days I was sometimes overwhelmed by feelings that convinced me once and for all that there was a deep rightness to the state of being alive. Standing on a windy mountaintop, seeing the clouds speeding over the waving trees, I suddenly felt my whole being moving and spreading with the general motion of nature. Or, lying lazily on a sunny meadow, high grasses and herbs camouflaging my persona from others and myself, I felt united with all creatures around me. These are not intelligent processes of cognition. Yet I am sure that the feelings of such moments are significant and, in a higher sense, true. Many people have similar experiences or visions. We should keep these "highs" or inspirations ready in our memory as a reserve of strength.

The meaning of life is not the domain of analyzing intelligence; meaning belongs to life alone. Consequently, whenever we have important decisions to make (about family matters, business, politics) we should ask ourselves: Is this action likely to advance life?

If this biosophical inquiry were to become a widespread habit, it would eventually produce an organic equilibrium of "spirit and flesh," as theologians used to call this dichotomy. It would finally establish a new and more solid balance—for life's sake.

5. Biosophical Sense

"My immortality is assured," said the dying spider. "Even while I will be hanging here dried out and immobile, my net will continue fulfilling its destiny of catching flies."

A man finds himself alone in an unknown, pitch black room. Vague menaces whirl around him; he thinks he could disperse them by looking sharply at them. He knows there must be a light switch on one of the walls, but where? If there were light in the room, he could find the switch immediately; but then, of course, he would not need it.

I believe that the meaning of life is immanent in life.

While being healthy, gainfully employed, or otherwise creative, participating in the concerns of a sympathetic milieu, an average person hardly ever gets the idea that his or her existence might be senseless. A normal life does not question itself. Usually, family and job are worth the trouble—even a lot of trouble.

During those recurrent periods when external order is stressed, the purpose of life is not allowed to be followed by a question mark. When the state assured the Hitler youths: "You are born in order to die for Germany," they had no further questions. In many historical situations the individual counts only insofar as he or she is part of a polarized crowd whose aims must be fulfilled with a high urgency; joining a group then has enough meaning in itself, since it augments the drive. This is the dark, seductive power of collective undertakings. Whenever a leader is sure that victory must be on the side of the larger batallions, a single person does not require special significance.

But when such superimposed purposes are fulfilled or defeated, discredited or out of fashion, individuals must think about their own tasks and create or select new aims for themselves. Breaking the mold is sometimes needed to reveal its hollowness. Suicide never occurs under undecided battle conditions.

Among the feelings and conditions inimical to the sense of "fullness of life," three seem to me especially pernicious because their negative influence is hardest to counteract by means of logical rationality. These three negations within the human psyche are the following:

First, the anticipation of death. You feel that nothing in life matters since everything will soon be annihilated by your dying and by your ceasing to participate.

Second, staleness, the lack of spice in your life, surfeit, paralysis of your vital spirits. This is the feeling which, as *taedium vitae,* held much of the late Roman civilization in its grip.

Third, fatalism, the feeling of lacking freedom: acceptance of inescapable *kismet* or *ananke.* You seem to be forced to act (or not to act) by invisible constrictions inherited from unknown forefathers, by a genetic code, by economic laws you don't understand, or simply by habit. Germans sometimes react with *Weltschmerz,* Frenchmen shrug their shoulders in *m'enfoutisme,* American behaviorists write learned books trying to prove that life is a determinate clockwork whirring away its pre-ordained span.

If we could defuse these three time bombs that menace life—death, tedium, and determinism—at least psychologically, the possibility to live for life's sake would become clearer and stronger.

Death is included in the contract when we enter life. It is not a surprise, not entirely foreign to life. Dying is a part of living, it is not something wild and incomprehensible. Dying never occurs where living did not precede; ergo it is an integral late phase of the wonderful process of living. A statue does not die; who, for this reason, would want to be a statue? Death does not invalidate life in retrospect; it rounds off our existence.

Besides, we can console ourselves with Epicure's dictum: "Death does not concern me. When I am here, he is not here; and when he is here, I am not here."

As a child I was dismayed when I learned that a certain species of fly emerges from the larval state without a mouth. These adult flies cannot eat! Even if they wished to live on after their final sex act, fate has made it impossible for them: Their front end is closed up. I was deeply shocked.

As I grew older, I got the impression that we are all traveling along a one-way lane that is, at the same time, a dead-end street. The childish larva that could still suck nourishment from the idea of eternity has burst its cocoon; now it can only digest the remaining concept of time. And when time has been broken down into its good juices and into the indigestible remainder—regrets and unfulfilled wishes—then the individual starts digesting itself, just as a freshly dead corpse digests its own stomach. There is no last-minute special delivery or deliverance. The front end is closed, and we'll be lucky to find a decent exit.

There is one comfort, which seems to grow stronger with ageing. In our children and further descendents the order of our chromosomes may continue to exist. Perhaps one gamete cell, guarding its identity, has escaped from mortality. You also may imagine that you'll live on in some precept or symbol that you have dispensed in your prime. Though logically, all this may be inconclusive, it helps psychologically. This is one of the few advantages of growing older.

What we object to when we shudder before death is not the state of not-being; nonexistence can really contain no menaces and horrors of which we might be afraid. Besides, we should be accustomed to this state—or, rather, nonstate—because in it we have already spent the unthinkably long period before our conception and birth. Death will only be a return to this comfortable (or at least neutral) oblivion.

We object to the terrifying, urgent menace that suddenly "our time is up." Time, so necessary to life, is also its enemy: a time-span carries its own annihilation within itself.

This unique instant, for instance: Never and nowhere in the world will it return, not in millions of years. Perhaps there are no millions of years? Perhaps there is always only the instant? Sometimes I think it must be only a willful decision that now is now. Wouldn't it be more beautiful to dance freely across the ocean of time?

Now. Now. It is always only now. How boring this can be! But occasionally I feel the opposite way, and I marvel that we can make the connection to other nows. How is this possible, since the past, strictly speaking, does not exist? Only the testimonials for the past are there, and these exist—now! Stone tablets, brittle bones, yellowed last wills: they are present, otherwise they would not be available to us. Have we been cheated out of our past?

Times passes—what should this mean? Am I sliding out from time into some untime? Am I no longer within "now"? This may be sophistry, but there is a kernel of truth in it. "Now" is the center of time, and I am right in this center. Geometrically, this instant is the middle between the immeasurable stretch called past and the future, which is just as immeasurably long. No matter where I establish this "now"-point, it is the heart of things and therefore of surpassing importance. And just as, in ancient times and foreign countries, a halfway-house served travelers who wished to change horses, to refresh themselves and rest before riding on, so we might as well relax and be of good cheer in the halfway-house we call our present.

Do you fear that with each passing day your life is becoming one day shorter? No, it is the other way around: your life has again become one day longer. Yesterday it was, for example, twenty-nine years long; today it measures twenty-nine years and a day. You can trust this strange arithmetic: in time's passing, there is no diminishing of time.

Wordsworth's life was longer than that of Keats, wasn't it? Your life is becoming longer, not shorter. An erroneous definition of time gives you an unjustified fright.

"Every day brings you closer to death": Isn't this the general opinion? Yet it's wrong. A shipwrecked sailor who survives the last day before his raft is discovered has improved his chances for a long life immensely: this one day has brought him farther away from death. A courageous patient clinging to life can still see the day when a new wonder drug or surgical feat might save her; a stubborn prisoner survives the death of a tyrant and is freed; a persecuted politician experiences the fall of his enemies' government. All these cases do not present exceptions from the pessimistic rule; they disprove the rule itself, they break it through progress, through brotherly love, or simply through lucky coincidence. It is not the passing of abstract time but the knot of concrete strands of events that produces each death. The insurance actuary earns his keep not through the average risks but through the exceptions therefrom.

Those who use a day—any day—to enrich their existence do not have to regret the passing of that day.

Undeniably there is a certain fascination in the feeling that our existence is provisory, and fatalism has a strange black radiance. But shaping our life serves to contradict the negative argument which death holds up to each of us.

Personally, I would be quite disappointed if I died of an incurable disease and if, a few weeks later, a remedy for this sickness were found.

The strongest enemy of life is not the clear, exactly circumscribed event of death, but the vague suspicion of aimlessness, lack of purpose, the absence of sense.

In decadent times, especially where there has been no recent upheaval of the social structure, this *taedium vitae* becomes a fashionable, almost snobbish attitude: Unesteemed wealth devalues the gifts of life. In epochs that have preserved an inner strength, this languor often leads to asceticism, to renouncing "the world." Romantic periods convert this frustration into nostalgia, suffering from the present state of the universe. This strong cultural strain runs from Goethe's "Werther," who induced many young people to seek suicide as a way out; to Wagner's "Tristan"; to the languid

French symbolists. This long and varied scale of denouncing and renouncing life may still be operative in some adaptations of Eastern religious thought to Western circumstances.

The statements of a person suffering from a surfeit of life have no truth-value; they communicate subjective sentiments, not objective knowledge. But whoever is plagued by this melancholy feels it with such power that it seems, to him, to give a true picture of the world and, therefore, to be irrefutable. "The end of one's tether" is, however, often not as stringent as it appears, and if one can hold out a few days or weeks, the constriction usually dissolves almost of its own accord. (Severe depressions, of course, demand medical treatment.)

An individual's potential to feel zest for life is not "more correct" than the disgust with life that perturbs so many people today. Logically and empirically, the experience of senselessness is no more justified than the—still far more prevalent—conviction that life is worth living. Neither the negative nor the positive attitude require any proof. Negativists think that they have seen through the maze of existence and that they can demonstrate the vanity and uselessness of all striving. But they never go beyond the temperamental, often-repeated assurance that they hate life and that we should do likewise. Contented or assiduous people can also never prove that they are right, that their knowledge of life reaches deeper than that of, say, a suicidal maniac or a fatalistic warrior.

However, one of my acquaintances once managed, by means of pure logic, to dissuade a friend bound for self-destruction: "Why go to all that trouble now—perhaps you'll be run over by a car next week, anyway." The potential suicide had to think about this long enough that his impetus became deflated, and he forgot his intention.

What do we really mean by the word "sense of life"? The evident fullness of life: an indubitable and concisely defined function of our fast-passing existence. Examples make this clear: a little girl absorbed by her play, a young couple during wooing and first fulfillment of love, a young mother suckling her baby, a diligent and well-paid family man, a scientist seeing a possible solution to a professional problem. They find themselves to be part of a functional order and, therefore, *making sense*. Senselessness, spleen, nausea come to the fore when life is no longer directed. A sense of life is generated in two situations: naively, in a structured, but not too tight net of reciprocal relations; and self-consciously, in taking stock from a higher perspective, as a creative act.

The sense or purpose a person feels within can be doubted and scoffed at by observers; but it can never be disproved, since it is only a function of this person's life. Purpose is not somewhere out there in the cold, colorless structure of the *Dinge an sich,* of "the things as such"; life must relate to itself in order to make sense.

In a well-balanced life, the two sensations "this seems senseless" and "that will bring me fulfillment" can become inner signals, a kind of traffic light of the soul.

Many attacks of moral philosophers and theologians condemning the senses originated in an amazing semantic mix-up. In pious treatises we read only of sensual lust, joy of the senses, devilish sensuousness. These writers appear not to have noticed that the sensation of pain is also produced through the senses; that ugliness is transmitted by the optical sense organs; that revulsion, shame, sorrow are correlated to or fed through impressions. The flagellant feels his penance with his tactile nerves.

We should talk about joy *and* pain of the senses to do justice to these phenomena. Thus we can eliminate the old puritanical prejudice against sensuality. We can find sense in our senses.

Instead of striving to give new depth to life, we tend to flatten it out more and more. No matter how complex and subtle a personality, for official use it is reduced to a very flat index card with holes punched in it.

This modern tendency to make everyday existence a platitude has produced vigorous reactions, some of them beneficial, some destructive. Mystical and religious revival groups have gained many adherents. Juveniles are attracted by the adventurous atmosphere of militancy, gangsterism, and drugs. Dangerous activities help them break out of the senselessness of the life cycle in our ugly megalopolis. They don't like to ask adults to show them what can be meant by meaning, the aims of church and state seem irrelevant or discredited, hard work on the job seems to add not values but pollution to the environment.

The basic difficulty of most adults to disperse young people's tedium with the establishment is that you cannot talk them out of it logically: They see the grown-ups pursue many varied aims, but rarely one overriding purpose on which everybody can agree. Living in a split-up, widely divergent culture, you can, at best, convince them in practical, day-to-day work. They would much rather have one preeminent goal, such as a revolution or some other total solution to all our woes. The sweeping, visionary generalization of one big task transforms some into radicals; others, lacking such a purpose, are tempted to escape into mystical or drug-oriented pseudo-solutions.

It has been observed that blind children like to press or knock on their useless eyeballs. After some scolding and studying, the supervising persons found out the reason: these children generate light in their brains. The optic nerves, never stimulated from the outside, still create their specific sensation when excited through pressure or beating, and this excitement is read by the brain as light.

People who consume hallucinogenic drugs don't realize how similar they are to these pitiful blind creatures who produce nonexistent light. Some of these children could have been operated on and their sight restored if they had not damaged their eyeballs by pursuing the wrong solution.

Next to adolescence (when tasks have not yet been stabilized "for life"), the retirement age is the most dangerous. All of a sudden the accustomed purposes have dried up. At sixty-five a healthy, relatively strong "senior citizen" is shut out from factory or office. Statistics show that the death rate among well-provided-for retired people jumps and becomes much higher than the mortality among hard-working oldsters. This danger lasts, on the average, one year, after which the mortality curve evens out. The "obsolete" human being needs a year to adjust to the freedom from exterior purposes; then life becomes, once again, worth the trouble.

Technological unemployment will not go away, it will make this dilemma ever more acute, regardless of economic cycles. The Protestant ethic considered work its own reward, leisure was justifiable only as preparation for renewed activity. More than one-third of every human's personal time was dedicated to super-imposed duties; almost one-third was consumed by sleep, anyway; it did not require special ingenuity to fill up the remaining one-third with necessary or pleasant tasks. But now, with more leisure than ever, the creation of purpose is more critical. We still cannot rid ourselves of the prejudice that laziness is the workshop of the devil. The term "unemployed" gives us a bad conscience. Why? To earlier centuries leisure was a privilege; aristocrats found satisfaction in hunting, art, court intrigues, feasting, and erotic games. A free citizen of antiquity or the Renaissance was proud not to make a living by the sweat of his brow. Today hobbies, sports, travel provide days and weeks of directedness. There are certainly enough tasks for volunteers in our polluted and littered environment. There is no doubt that we can adapt ourselves to the necessity of establishing our own purpose. The proposition that anybody could really have too much time seems quite unrealistic.

Human beings usually have a surplus of vital energy. If this excess is not consumed or destroyed by famine, pestilence, and war, the governing authorities like to use it up for crusades, vast construction projects, moving enormous masses of men and materiel. Pyramids, cathedrals, space flights are among the more sensible undertakings. To let people just live their lives is a waste in the eyes of the leaders. Directors have acquired their positions because of their busy-ness and will-power, and once having attained command they cannot switch off this initiative; so they invent aims that lead beyond the usual everyday activities of disorganized, messy masses.

Such polarized enterprises are advanced by a definite predilection of homo sapiens for directional motions: Circular movements of living beings seem senseless to us, one-way movements are almost dogmatically supposed to make sense. The slave who turns a treadmill with always equal steps has to be coerced. Assembly lines are reaching a point of diminishing returns. The manager sees their directedness, but the worker feels their repetitions as circular and therefore devoid of sense. Straight-line efforts are furthered unhesitatingly, more willingly and easily, and it is of secondary importance whether these directed efforts are fruitful or a waste of energy. You are "carried away" only by one-sided motions, and this makes the initial enthusiasm for the most dreadful incursions understandable. The arrow, as a directional sign, as a weapon, or even as an ornament in art, is most congenial to the human psyche.

We could utilize this vectorial quality of our mind much more efficiently to further our living standard and our culture. Do we really need the often grotesque extravaganzas—luxurious palaces, princely jubilees, crusades—to call us to concentrated displays of energy? Could we not generate similar enthusiasm to clean up our dumpy neighborhoods, to convert slums and favelas into dignified dwelling places, to conquer sickness and hunger? Instead of promoting boxing matches we could schedule sanitation campaigns with exact time limits, with circumscribed financial, localized planning: we could realize sober, "normal" aims in one all-out effort. What is discouraging in such matters is the endless, halfhearted application of stopgap measures in recurrent patterns. A government or an ad hoc agency should proclaim one improvement festival for a particular part of one city; this should be renovated with the combined efforts of all concerned, with the promise that afterwards the inhabitants would have their privacy again, while a new slum clearance festival for a different part of town is prepared.

The eminently American institution of the "drive" has been utilized for selling war-bonds, for mass inoculations, for eradicating pests. Why not use it to combat illiteracy, drug abuse or, say, cigaret smoking? Human willpower is geared to attain clearly circumscribed aims in an exactly prescribed period of time.

This directional quality of human life is indeed what connects us with the biological development from primitive to sophisticated forms.

As we have seen, the doctrine of the preservation of mass and energy is not valid for the psyche and its projections. From this it follows that outgoing, joyous people do not consume their inner beings faster than those who are cautious, reticent, sulky. The spirit emerges from the circulatory life processes without being fettered by this tiresome circle game. This in turn means that it is more gratifying to let one's spirit roam freely, to be interested and to participate in many concerns, than to capsulate oneself in misanthropic isolation. The dullard saves nothing, not even himself. Only by losing yourself, by abandoning yourself to living aims, can you win yourself.

Are we free?

Rousseau said: "Man was born free, but everywhere he is bound in chains." The concept of freedom has in itself such latent explosive power that its mere naming sometimes suffices to generate enthusiastic actions and sacrifices. But ordinarily, when we talk of liberty, we don't mean something absolute: Practical freedom is what people wish for. Certain rights of fellow citizens have to be respected; no one wants the liberty to drive through a red traffic light or to shout "fire!" in a crowded theater. People want special liberties: choice between various methods of production and consumption, political freedom of assembly and speech, self-determination for a tribe, class, sect, or nation.

Behind all these allowances for partial freedom lurks a disquieting question: Are we, in principle, able to choose freely—is not every so-called decision already predetermined by existing causations? If the basic freedom of the will is not given to mankind, what good are limited choices and liberal concessions in special situations?

Thus the problem is reduced to the age-old, much-discussed dilemma of whether or not we are capable of free volition.

Fatum, kismet, predestination by divine grace: These compulsive fantasies may today have melted into the general pot of superstition. (I want to avoid discussing astrological predetermination and occult influences on our actions: In spite of their fashionable resurrection, they are too far removed from the scope of our inquiry.) The most reputable attack on the freedom principle comes from the most exact natural sciences.

For instance, Dean E. Wooldridge writes: "Free will poses no problem—it simply doesn't exist."[23] That is a succinct statement. But it leaves unexplained why it is necessary to condemn "free will": Is there, in contrast, an unfree will? If we have any will at all, it must be free. Wooldridge maintains: "The purely physical properties of the neuronal structures are adequate, without further stimulus than that provided by the outside environment, to result automatically in such intellectual actions as considering, deciding, directing, reviewing, and choosing."[24] Consequently, he calls man a machine.

Spinoza wrote in honest equanimity: "Freedom is the acceptance of necessity."

In 1748, David Hume stated:

However we imagine we feel a liberty within ourselves, a spectator can commonly infer our actions from our motives and character; and even where he cannot, he concludes in general that he might, were he perfectly acquainted with every circumstance of our situation and temper, and the most secret springs of our complexion and disposition. Now this is the very essence of necessity.[25]

When we try to alter our action and, upon repetition, to select a different course, the fantastical wish to prove our freedom is the cause of our new and different action. Thus Hume votes for inescapable determinacy.

As the patron saint of the determinists, Buridan's ass is enthroned to preside over the discussion. This good animal, probably invented by Jean Buridan in Paris before 1350, still stands in the exact middle between two equally attractive sheaves of hay and suffers the pangs of hunger without being able to choose. An incredibly asinine behavior! Konrad Lorenz gives us the supplementary information that a radar-directed rocket will fly between two airplanes if both targets appear on the screen symmetrically. He further relates that goldfish catch fewer waterfleas if too many are offered simultaneously: Their power of decision wanes, confronted by too many temptations. But it seems to me that this signifies only that sometimes choice is difficult, not that there is no possiblity of free choice.

In "real life" Buridan's ass won't die of hunger, he will decide. We never hear of animals or men starving within reach of food. An iron ball, placed on a certain spot between two magnets, may remain immobile. But we are not iron objects, we are not stable systems. Life processes are directional. Buridan's friend may decide for the sheaf on his right because he is right-footed, or because his last step before reaching the central spot happened to be taken with his left foot. Even if all his impulses should be in equilibrium for several seconds, his inner organs, his blood circulation, or his nervous system will send out an asymmetrical stimulus: He himself, the exemplary ass, will then have decided, without any outward cause.

Perhaps he chooses the hay on his right because a gas bubble wanders through his intestines and causes him discomfort, from which he then turns away. Does this flatus belong to his person (if we can call him a person)? Then it is he who decides, that's clear. But can gas be an integral part of an ass? Perhaps not. Then did an external cause influence his choice? On the other hand: His intestine belongs to his organism! The "I" is not a physical concept, its effective radius changes from one action to the next; yet, in the aforementioned predicament, the painful flatus is certainly part of the ass's conscious ego.

Is this example too earthbound for philosophical speculation? Very often it is just such stuff from which our decisions are made.

Some motives may derive from the sublime love of the true, beautiful, and good; most causes are quite prosaic.

To come back to our quadruped: Even the most rigid determinist must admit that nobody can really predict whether Buridan's ass, starting from a balanced position, will choose the left or the right bundle of hay; to do so, the experimenter would have to introduce electrodes or the like into the animal's skull in order to read his thoughts and to follow the genesis of his decision. With these electrodes attached, the ass might decide otherwise than he would have done without them. Does this difficulty seem familiar? If an experiment is influenced by the process of observation, physicists do not accept it as conclusive. (This was at the root of Heisenberg's principle of uncertainty.) Self-fulfilling prophecies are usually considered to be cheating, and rightly so.

David Hume was convinced that we can learn everything important about human behavior from scrutinizing history. Hume wrote:

The same motives always produce the same actions: The same events follow from the same causes. Ambition, avarice, self-love, vanity, friendship, generosity, public spirit: These passions, mixed in various degrees, and distributed through society, have been, from the beginning of the world, and still are, the source of all the actions and enterprises, which have ever been observed among mankind.

Hume's determinism goaded him into making imprudent predictions.

Should a traveller, returning from a far country, bring us an account of men, wholly different from any with whom we were ever acquainted; men who were entirely divested of avarice, ambition, or revenge; who knew no pleasure but friendship, generosity, and public spirit; we should immediately, from these circumstances, detect the falsehood, and prove him a liar, with the same certainty as if he had stuffed his narration with stories of centaurs and dragons, miracles and prodigies.

A report on the peaceful Hunza people would have been declared *a priori* unbelievable by the Scottish philosopher. He would also have rejected as a fable any description of the Semai in

Malaysia, who never apply corporal punishment to their children and to whom murder is unknown.

Hume's trouble was that he did not really think in causal terms —though he was convinced that he did—but in a predicative way: a very common mistake. If we ascribe certain predicates or properties to a living being, we believe that we have defined and explained its character and, consequently, its behavior. This, however, is putting the cart before the horse; or rather, before Buridan's ass.

Here's how this faulty process works: We observe and register different actions of a particular individual. From these we formulate his peculiarities and qualities, and after that we ascribe them as permanent attributes to his essential being. Then, from these supposedly static properties, we prophesy with certainty his future actions and behavior. This flimsy calculus, which uses constant attributes, becomes especially dangerous when it seems to confirm our expectations for a while: This may often be only a sign that the individual in question has been forced, by being formulated, into his expected role.

This inductive thinking becomes completely unreliable if it deals with such complicated entities as provincial parts of nations, social classes, religious splinter groups. Not even a seemingly clear-cut label such as "feminine qualities" can be used to predict concrete female behavior: There will always be women whose character won't fit into the conventional pigeonholes. Their actions may confuse and dismay male critics, but not for long—the males will formulate yet another "definition" of femininity and, at the next opportunity, misuse it.

Determinists insist that the rigidly repetitive nature of all our actions and reactions permits predictions of our future behavior. Hume was convinced that an observer can predict our actions from our motives and from our character. This expectation would carry more weight if Hume, who had studied "the" French character, would have prophesied from it that the French Revolution would occur only thirty years later. He didn't. Nobody predicted it.

German animal psychologists recently daubed green paint on the white feathers of a seagull. The animal, which no longer falls under the concept "white seagull," was hacked to death by its friends and relatives.

Man has introduced the reverse procedure: Varied individuals are all colored the same by putting military uniforms on them. This conceptual sleight-of-hand generates the same attributes and characteristics in the dressed-up soldiers. They themselves, their superiors, and their enemies then expect them to act alike in different offensive and defensive situations. Finally, each one of them is forced to fulfill these expectations—whether or not they correspond to his or her real character—and standardized aggressiveness prevails.

The most effective attack on our freedom of choice stems from behaviorism, especially from B. F. Skinner. On the basis of successful animal training, especially of rats and pigeons, Skinner proposed that somebody should also lead humans to their salvation through operant conditioning. For this purpose he would have us renounce freedom and dignity.

In Skinner's theories, the wish is the father of the thought: His drive to manipulate people takes precedence over his scientific observations. This becomes clear from a remark he made in 1953 before his doctrine became world-famous.

If we are to use the methods of science in the field of human affairs, we must assume that behavior is lawful and determined. We must expect to discover that what a man does is the result of specifiable conditions and that once these conditions have been discovered, we can anticipate and to some exent determine his actions.[26]

Consequently, Skinner recommends programmed education, controlled environment, conditioned reactions in every facet of life. A dismal outlook.

The various doctrines that espouse the possibility of aimed developments in this world are usually lumped together under the term "teleology." Today, teleological dogmata, intimations, or inklings are rejected as mystical by most natural scientists. Any idea that an end can preshape a development is negated or ignored. The neo-Darwinians in particular have denied all explanations of forms by their purpose. An eye, they say, exists not for seeing; rather, it sees because it happens to exist.

Alfred North Whitehead made fun of these physiologists and psychologists:

Many a scientist has patiently designed experiments for the *purpose* of substantiating his belief that animal operations are motivated by no purpose. He has perhaps spent his spare time in writing articles to prove that human beings are as other animals so that "purpose" is a category irrelevant for the explanations of their bodily activities, his own activities included. Scientists animated by the purpose of proving that they are purposeless constitute an interesting subject for study.[27]

Meanwhile, "purpose-free" science has become even more influential.

That we are teleological beings—that our thoughts and movements are best understood when they are considered not only as causally motivated but also as purpose-oriented—I can demonstrate by the following physiological observation. The human eye moves, typically, only quickly and jerkily. If you try to let your gaze roam slowly across the sky in a constant motion, you'll find soon that this does not work: The eye movement will get stuck in short intervals. If, however, you move your index finger in a leisurely sweep across the sky and stare at its moving tip, your eyes will follow it in a smooth constant motion. (You can verify this by having the sun within your field of vision: The after-image forms a knotted, interrupted line in the first case; a clean, even line in the second.) If the eye sets for itself the purpose of following a traveling automobile, it moves evenly; if it wanders aimlessly through a room, it sticks to a hundred points and corners. Two very different modes of behavior.

This proves that the eye is not directed by the eye muscles but by its seeing—that is, by its object, by its purpose. The eye behaves in an aimed fashion, that is, teleologically! The same holds true for the working hands: the left and the right hand are activated by completely different sets of muscle contractions, and yet they can reach, interchangeably, the same aim.

The end directs the action. Purposeful behavior has possibilities and laws which are different from the "useless," relaxed intervals. *Humans can conduct themselves very sensibly.*

This also applies to animals. Biological experiments have shown that the presentiment of an aim is decisive. For instance, a rat was taught to avoid dead ends and detours in a maze. Later, the maze was put under water to let the rat swim toward its target. Every single motion of muscle and limb now had to be different, and yet the rat reached its cheese without any hesitation. This proves that the rat's muscular movements had not been conditioned as reflexes to various landmarks; only its spirit had been programmed. Even this poor rat behaved not in a causal, but in a final way; and should not scientists do the same?

It is not the mechanics of our organs which command our life, but vice versa. After a coronary heart attack the blood creates a new path for itself, avoiding the damaged artery and widening smaller blood vessels. You can describe this causally, if you wish; however, a description starting from the side of the purpose is more adequate to the natural facts.

This has nothing whatever to do with entelechies or providence. The body regenerates itself for life's sake. We live for life's sake.

Teleology and causality are not incompatible. The development of a seed into a tree can be described in causal terms through elucidation of all pertinent biochemical processes: a very complicated description, but possible. The same development can be expressed in equally logical terms through the image of an aim contained in the seed: The acorn realizes the prefigured *gestalt* of the adult oak tree; it executes the project while slumbering inside its capsule. No matter if the roots meet stones, loam, air pockets, or sand—they feel their way, advancing through the underground until they have reached their approximate symmetry on all sides. Compared to the interior purpose, the exterior influences are almost ineffective.

In homo sapiens this feedback is even more distinct than in a tree: An imagined end becomes the cause of our actions—what Aristotle called the "final cause."

The sequence "always when, then" is considered the sign of a causal relation. Is this a reliable connection? *Always* when the town hall clock strikes eight, then Mr. Johnston enters his office. This would appear to be an inductive lawfulness. Yet the physiological causes of Johnston's action are different each day: Once he has eaten an egg for breakfast, which replenished his reserves of strength; another time a kippered herring has given him the necessary impetus. One time he walked, another time he took a bicycle: two entirely different causal chains. The aim–image, the will to arrive at the office at eight o'clock, was the motive behind his action. The physiochemical causal connection was unimportant to the result.

An end, as idea, sense-data, or "attractive" suggestion, can become the cause of an action, of a development: Causality and finality supplement each other. Thus emerges a multiple, inexhaustibly fascinating pattern on the loom of life: The warp threads are stretched out from the past, they are the given facts in the time dimension; the woof of purpose crosses these connections to form a significant web.

We could go on discussing these matters theoretically, as has been done for centuries, if a practical application did not urgently demand a shortcut: This is the problem of responsibility. The everyday dispensing of justice demands that a criminal be judged as speedily as feasible, and that the extent of his or her guilt be circumscribed and fitted with the appropriate punishment. At this point the vague feeling of responsibility must be quantified: so much money, so much time must be exacted from the guilty party. Therefore ethical doctrines must be translated into social rules.

Twentieth-century justice asks in almost every criminal case: Has the criminal acted freely or under duress? If he planned his deed coolly in advance deliberation, then it is his deed. If a compulsive neurosis caused his action, he is not quite as responsible and, therefore, less punishable.

This distinction is not a rational one. If you lock up the neurotic, you therewith lock up his neurosis, thus punishing the guilty part. But bare rationality cannot be the decisive factor here; humaneness is more important, the possibility of healing must be guaranteed, the probability of backsliding, the danger for the fellow-citizens must be weighed.

The new liberal atmosphere first manifested itself most strongly in the 1924 murder case of Leopold and Loeb, when the famous lawyer Clarence Darrow pleaded for mitigating circumstances: "What has this boy to do with it [the murders he committed]? He was not his own father; he was not his own mother; he was not his own grandparents. He did not make himself. And yet he is to be compelled to pay." Darrow won that case, and since then jurisprudence has had to limit the stark principle of responsibility.

If Darrow was right, if no person can be held responsible for his or her actions because their causations can be traced back before the birth of the doer, then nobody could receive a Nobel prize, for the inherited qualities were not his or her merit. Normally, however, an adult in average health and practical freedom has enough possibility to display his willpower so that he, his own person, is a decisive link in the causal chain.

Many juridical prescriptions for the treatment of humans—instruction, forced reparations, deterrence, cure, castration, torture, physical elimination—were and still are rejected or recommended by professionals and laypeople without end. Justice will be defined differently in different times and climes. These are practical problems. Theoretically, the question of causation seems to grow more important.

If a person who has a revolver aimed at him is forced to perform a certain action, he is not considered responsible, even though his giving in to threats may really have been a flaw in his character. If the revolver is within him, so-to-speak, in the guise of fanaticism, chauvinism, family allegiance to gangsterism, his responsibility is discussed and weighed. If the revolver is part of his personality—if he designates himself as a professional revolutionary, if he is a paid murderer or a person constitutionally lacking any moral feeling—

society isolates or destroys the menace together with his person. Being a murderer has gradual differences, according to the inner and outer compulsions. It is not a static quality which somebody has or has not, once and for all.

Here the somewhat old-fashioned concept of "a strong personality" comes into play.

Michelangelo was the cause of his creations; who could deny this? That the Medici and Pope Julius II ordered these works, thus causing their existence in the narrowest sense, is secondary when it comes to distributing merits.

This, however, is denied by behaviorists. I once saw Professor Skinner during a televised interview when he grew somewhat tired and let sentences slip out that he might have censored while writing quietly at his desk. The question was asked whether any random person, brought into Michelangelo's exact circumstances, would have produced the same works of art. "Without any doubt," quoth Skinner, and continued talking about something else.

I am firmly convinced that determinism—the "always when, then" complex—does not play an appreciable part in important human actions. The numerous old and new contestations concerning psychological determinism can be condensed into three principal objections.

First objection: The causal row "always when, then" is incapable of verification in human beings. Examination could only take place through repetition. But when one action is repeated the acting person is a little older and perhaps not so interested; the engrams in his cerebral cortex of the first execution cannot be erased, his motives are colored differently by the fact of repetition: Too many new causes and stimuli enter the experimental field to permit us to call it the same action. Serial reactions can be accomplished in sterile test tubes, or, perhaps, in rat cages; but not in human life. It just cannot be scientifically maintained that a person will always react in the same way to the same causes. The thesis "always when, then" does not fall apart in the conclusion, but in the premise: There is no "always when" that comprises all the relevant circumstances. The Greek saying, "You cannot step twice into the same river" concerns not only the changeable river; the "you" is also never the same twice.

Ergo: There simply is no 100 percent certain prediction of human behavior.

Second objection against psychological determinism: The "I" is flexible. The I absorbs, anew at each action, various causes; it becomes as a whole, including many earlier causes, the doer. If later on it wants to reject and throw out some of these causes—if, for instance, it says that it only acted on superior orders—we have to reply that, initially, the receptivity for orders from higher-up must have been an effective part of the I-structure; otherwise the I would not have reacted to and absorbed that initial order. Responsibility, as an aura of the individual I, changes with every deed; but whether it be larger or smaller, in every case it belongs to the personality. Ergo: We are responsible for our—good and bad—actions.

Third objection to the idea that our psyche is determinate through outer circumstances: Causality and predetermination are not the same principles. Human actions are not predeteminate even if we acknowledge (as we must) that the law of cause and effect is inescapably valid (in our median, terrestrial reaches). For predicting or predetermining, a total picture of all the facts would be needed, and this cannot be accomplished. To anticipate single events, it does not suffice to know general laws; it also does not suffice to know one concept under which several single data can be subsumed; one would have to know each individual fact that has influenced the causal web at any time, including the future.

This would mean a complete duplication of the world in one human brain, which is patently impossible (except for a world spirit, and he would then be identical with nature, as Spinoza supposed).

At this juncture, the principle of uncertainty is usually introduced. The physicist Werner Heisenberg proved more than half a century ago that we never know exactly at which point an electron is located if we know how fast this electron is moving, and vice versa: We can know either its location or its speed. Natural scientists agree that this indeterminacy is not the fault of the description, but that it shows an impossibility in principle. If a thing can never be verified, it cannot be the object of a scientific statement.

Similarly, it is impossible for us to determine the future course of a human life; and this, apart from the question as to whether the law of causality does or does not determine that life. We must not proclaim what we cannot verify. Even if we function in a causal fashion, we don't, therefore, function in a predictable or predetermined way.

Ergo: we cannot be programmed.

Thus the age-old antinomy between free will and causal captivity is resolved and the problem solved. We can rely on our theoretical freedom. And this should *cause* us to rejoice!

Our precious personal feeling of being free has been attacked from various quarters at different times. Formerly, it was the belief in predestination through demonic and divine powers: This superstition was ordained or dethroned in regular cycles. Toward the end of the nineteenth century the idea of inherited compulsions exerted an almost hypnotic pull. It was believed that character traits and degenerate flaws of our ancestors foredoomed our own biographies. This *leitmotivic* determination, which held whole series of novels together (Zola's, for instance), is today considered a minor problem. After that, economic determinacy was thought to be inescapable; this idea, too, has lost its scientific reputation.

It is true that inherited genes, family diseases, hereditary aptitudes can influence humans from the inside while, from the outside, economic, spiritual, military organizations try to sway personal decisions. But it is not true that one set of causations excludes the other. After all, influences only lead to individual choices if a person's character is open to such intrusions. This means that the individual is an integral link in a causal chain, that no decision can be arrived at without consent.

If you depend too much on the supposition that people in equal situations act the same each time, you may be in for some disagreeable surprises. This happened to an Austrian emperor. One day he was informed: "Your Majesty, the burghers are making a revolution." The emperor replied, in bewilderment: "Revolution? Well, are they allowed to do that?"

There are no frightful, no noble actions that human beings have not undertaken now and then. In various epochs you can rely, respectively, on their submissiveness or on their will to liberation, on innate goodness or on character-warping through the suggestion of total depravity, on economic causation or private initiative or rational planning—whatever the times, systems, or mental fashions require; in other periods such rules become unreliable, and whoever tries to operate politically or economically with such behavioral standards is bound to receive rude disappointments.

All this is pretty obvious, except to dogmatic partisans of one school of thought or another.

But there is one further factor in human behavior that makes causality practically unimportant. To wit: Every person has a fund of energy within that can release—not cause—an action. The trigger on a rifle does not give the bullet its penetrative force; it only sends it on its way. Similarly, a tender, thoughtful, even weak motive, put into play at the right spot, can initiate gigantic effects.

The decisive phenomenon is that the I-structure can, in an almost spongelike fashion, suck up causes from its surroundings and make them its own motives, thus changing the I itself. The experiences and instructions we receive from the outside become integral parts of our personalities. A student of physics may get his working methods, views, and hypotheses from an older professor; these will help him only if he absorbs and integrates them into his personality; and if, twenty years later, he receives the Nobel prize, it is not his teacher but he himself who has earned it.

William James describes how he was lying in bed on an icy winter morning and could not make up his mind to get up; no motive to excite his will was strong enough, only in principle did he want to arise. Later on he discovered that he had gotten up without thinking, without an act of volition or an impulse that could be defined in time.

In similar circumstances, I did a little introspecting myself. When I resolved in the evening to wake up especially early the next morning, I found that I absorbed outer motivations to accomplish this. Still asleep, I heard a rooster crowing; half asleep, I heard the clatter of milk bottles outside my door, and so on. I would not have taken notice of these small disturbances if I had not imprinted the wish to get up early into various facets of my brain, including the aural sense organs. My will used these causations to effect my own decision, I did not act causally but in a final manner. I, not the milkman, was responsible for my getting up early.

Like a reflection in a gallery of mirrors, the exact point where willpower attacks reality becomes the more elusive the harder we look. This is the difficulty when we think causally. But as soon as we turn our manner of observing around and start thinking from the aim, from the end—which means, as soon as we judge the row of psychological states before the event as directional—the trouble disappears, and the individual volition becomes clear and persuasive.

Is this only a philosophical legerdemain? Hardly; it is indeed impossible to think back causally through the web of circumstances until we reach a *prima causa*. There is no single, definite juncture of will and things that would not be preceded by many motives. But the I of the doer is the cause of the deed, because this I absorbs and contains those motives.

The fund of mental energy an individual starts amassing as a child is, doubtlessly, part of his or her *I*, even during times when this energy is not manifest. Causality in a person functions not like the aforementioned billiard balls; it is all translated and mirrored in projections. The hidden fund or storage of character strength, knowledge, and reserves of willpower can be deployed as a surprise to everyone, including one's enemies. What's more: an educator or a good government can utilize this fund in entirely new directions that were previously outside the ken of that particular individual.

Possibilities like these make the apostle of free will seem friendlier, more philanthropic, and more optimistic than the advocate of fatalism.

The senselessless of compulsive actions can sometimes be amusing. For centuries a Russian soldier appeared every morning in the park of Zarskoye Selo palace to do guard duty on a certain spot. One guard relieved the other day after day, year after year. Only after the 1917 revolution someone inquired why this empty spot on the lawn was worthy of a special guard. It was discovered that Empress Catharine the Great had once seen a violet blooming there and had ordered a soldier to protect the flower. The soldier, after fulfilling his duty for many years, had died; his successor died too. Nobody asked questions, the waste of human life went on unchecked, and the violet smiled down on the foolish humans from its special violet-heaven.

How many of our rites, manners, and laws go back to similar, long-since wilted, violets of the empress? How many empty formulas prevent us from using our free volition?

Another example: In 1919, during the German social-democratic revolution, a troop of revolutionaries wanted to occupy a Berlin railway station. The official at the platform gate, as is usual in Europe, stopped the wild-looking fellows: "You cannot enter here without a platform ticket." The men bought tickets, the official punched a hole into every card, and the revolution was allowed to proceed.

The theoretical discussion about free will versus determinism may seem irrelevant, seeing how often freedom is concretely hindered in many countries. Where the press is shackled and the opposition incarcerated, where hunger is used for leverage to enforce conformity, where reforms are called treason: there freedom must appear as a very solid, desirable good. Nonetheless, if the basic theory is flawed, some practical improvements may be deemed impossible or will be discouraged.

Only if we can consider ourselves as endowed with *free will* can we call on help from people of *good will*.

We have found that the three enemies of the sense of a full life—namely, anticipation of death, tedium, and mechanical predestination—can be circumscribed and confined to their proper places in the natural scheme of things. They are not overwhelming phantoms that should cause us to spend our existence in unceasing depression and fear.

Our time is *our* time.

Man is the measure and the center of his world. Our entire cultural history has lasted perhaps only twelve thousand years, which amounts to one-hundred-thousandth of life's existence on earth. Does this make it a negligible phenomenon? Not at all. Let's turn the argument around: The "lifespan" of certain radioactive elements is measured in one-thousandths of a second; if we compare these minuscule stretches to our own history, our concerns should appear immeasurably more important. Indeed, they are important—to ourselves, regardless of their duration.

Every day you experience brings an awakening, activities, disappointments, and satisfactions. In the evening you may wish to stay up longer, to finish an important output, or to receive some amusing input. You combat drowsiness; with some energy, you may be able to conquer it for a few hours. But then the black wall rises in front of you and becomes insurmountable. So you curl up, declaring a moratorium for all your concerns. An unlimited continuum of wakefulness is not permitted and not even desirable.

Similarly, life is a waking-up between two infinitely long periods of sleep. After an unimaginably long time in deepest limbo you open your eyes, slowly adapting to the waking state. You are confused and amazed by the world's crashing and twittering noises, by its changes of temperature from motherly warmth to cruel cold and hurtful heat. You almost believe that being awake is the normal state of affairs and might even last forever, just as the previous state of being submerged in lifelessness seems, in retrospect, to have lasted forever. This expectation is soon disproved rationally, and you become accustomed to the knowledge that you have to sink back into slumber at some yet undetermined point in time.

But you go on living, often in drowsy inattention. You seek some pastime, the passing of your only time.

If we could only use to the utmost those hours of wakefulness, looking out with wide-open eyes, plumbing as clearly as possible our own inner depths, making each brain cell and each muscle function joyfully and actively; if we could only perceive the whirling crowds around us, together with ourselves, as parts of an integrated organism called humanity; if we could seek and enjoy nature as help and wonder; if we could acknowledge the full value of the outer world, which depends on the perception of our senses and whose quality must disappear again when we close our eyes and ears for the second sleep; if we could maintain a state of heightened wakefulness at least for the decisive periods of our own time: Then our whole life would be worth the trouble—all the trouble.

What, then, can we do?

I have indicated by what strange tricks the human spirit can unfold an almost limitless power. If we acknowledge furthermore that we have a far-reaching capacity to freely apply our will, immense possibilities for efficiency result. The spirit—and here I mean the cool intellect—must augment the species' chances for survival by digesting the dangerous heritage of drives we carry deep inside our brains—or rather, in our guts.

The most tenacious among these primitive drives may be the sense of territory. Jean-Jacques Rousseau declared that the first man to drive a stake into the earth's surface in order to fence off private property was the originator of all social evils. To the modern prophets of the "territorial imperative," this drive seems both natural and beneficial. Yet the existence of nomadic peoples who live healthy and satisfying lives without being bound to a piece of soil disproves this claim. Our closest relative among the animals, the chimpanzee, has been shown by Jane Goodall to be nomadic.

This animal builds a nest in a tree for a peaceful night, abandons it in the morning with equanimity, and moves on to a different part of the forest.

The presumed divine, dynastic, juridic, or inherited right to a certain piece of land has caused more bloodshed than any other motive. Property radiates a mystical attraction; real estate sometimes seems the only wealth worthy of the attribute "real." In a wholly irrational way, soil is felt to be German soil, Jewish soil, Arab soil, or whatever. The land itself seems to have the characteristics of a national psyche—*deutsche Erde* appeared more romantic, honest, proud, and productive than "outlandish" territories. Rupert Brooke, who died as a soldier in World War I, rhapsodized: "If I should die, think only this of me: / That there's some corner of a foreign field / That is for ever England." The poor fool.

Territories once were worth conquering, driving out, or killing off the inhabitants; this, rationally, is no longer justified. An epoch that can erect high-rise buildings need not think in terms of flat stretches of land. People's lives now include the vertical dimension. When humans live and work in three-story houses, the inhabitability of a territory has increased threefold. This multiplication does not appear on maps, therefore groups continue contending for parts of the earth's surface. The same holds true for agricultural areas: the yield of a small, well-managed plot can be the multiple of an old-fashioned farm, but this is not expressed on maps either. Yet it is much more important—and much less dangerous—to utilize the available ground intensively than to press extensive claims. Just because Neanderthal man had no fertilizers, no water pipes, and no steel-frame building techique, our territorial instincts must not ignore recent developments. The brain's cortex must conquer its deeper and older layers.

Canine males mark their territorial claims by squirting urine; human males mark their conquests by shedding blood. I wonder which is more sensible.

Good clear thinking, without prejudices, can make us feel at home in the world. Once before, under the Roman empire with its *pax romana,* the citizens had become mobile, and everywhere

around the Mediterranean they could say: *Ubi bene ibi patria*—
"where it's good for me, there is my fatherland." Today the individual is not forced to rely on one certain ancestral cave into which
he has to retreat to ward off menaces.

Supplementary to the ancient territorial greed, we still harbor a
deep-seated fear of encirclement. Playing on this fear has fueled
many an arms race and war. A rat that has been cornered in a
backyard is driven into a state of wildly aggressive panic; a spar-
row, however, continues pecking at scraps or insects and only
gives the human intruder sidelong glances. Since 1871, when the
first balloon escape was accomplished out of beleaguered Paris, the
menacing, compulsory aspect of territoriality has dissolved more
and more. The Berlin airlift of 1949 was the definite demonstra-
tion of three-dimensional liberation. This trend, will, no doubt,
continue; and the magical power of borderlines drawn on maps
and of frontier markers will diminish.

Many of those traditional "rules of the game" can be softened
and rendered harmless by subjecting them to cool cogitation. How
about the blind, absolute loyalty to one's group? This arose because it was needed in a specific situation. The bond that made
prehistoric communities successful was the unquestioning acceptance of all purposes pursued by a restricted group within a tribe.
When hunters wanted to catch a mammoth or a rhinoceros in a
pit, driving the huge beast toward the trap and killing it required
the strictest cooperation among all participants. The membership
of each hunting party had to be numerically restricted so that the
hunters would stay within sight and earshot of each other. With
today's communication systems, this restrictiveness no longer has
a clear purpose. All kinds of conglomerations can be efficiently
organized, and their size does not have to stop even at nation-
states: The group can comprise the whole of humanity without
losing its cohesion. The modern "we," with all its connotations,
must surpass the "we" of our Neanderthal heritage.

The cohesiveness of a flock or herd was easily enforced; expul-
sion from the group meant almost unbearable hardship and probable death in the surrounding wilderness and "outer darkness."
These conditions, too, have changed in a fundamental way. Ex-

communication from the fold is not so deadly nowadays. We have more leeway, more choices.

Hunting groups had to rely on the predictability of their members' actions and attitudes: Their reactions to each challenge had to be the same every time. They had to trust that dangers, deprivations, and recompenses were distributed according to a fixed key that was defined as just. This must have produced social contracts even earlier than moral codes. Later on, moral tenets were formulated as binding for an entire tribe, later for a nation or sect, and they were enforced with utmost rigor.

Still, the progressive widening of behavioral systems never led to a worldwide code of absolute moral precepts. Shortly after Christian missionaries put clothes over the brown breasts of African and Polynesian women, white breasts in Europe and America began tanning in the sun. Matriarchal societies found it natural that women should have several husbands, while patriarchal tribes stoned adulteresses to death. Infanticide, a necessary ritual for some peoples, was a capital crime for others.

Montaigne complained about this variability of values: "What should be *the good* which received credit yesterday, but not tomorrow, and which, after you cross a river, turns into a crime? What kind of truth is that which is limited by these hills and which is considered error on the other side of the mountains?"

The wanderlust of the nineteenth century brought exact observations of the divergent *mores* and laws and among so-called primitive tribes. The earlier revulsion caused by deviations was given up, albeit hesitatingly, in the twentieth century. The collected anthropological data led to an almost complete relativization of moral philosophy. But, after all, we don't deny the findings of our astronomers even though we know that astronomic world views have been turned upside down and shattered several times within a few centuries.

We have to avow that morality, even when it was considered only as a loose guideline, was in existence always and everywhere. In every cultural group the individual who violated the established *mores* was called "immoral" and punished. Supposedly lawless gangsters and robbers are especially harsh in maintaining their own ethical code. Thieves' honor is, in its own way, more reliable than some dusty statutes of an honest citizenry.

Thinking in ever wider groupings and concerns, we come to the surprising conclusion that there is a certain ethical absoluteness: Not the old "thou-shalt-not" absolutism, but the requirement of reliable rules for humans to deal with each other. You can't play tennis without a net. The service of life for life's sake must be the key to any viable ethical system.

In one important respect, we should trust nature much more than people have done for the last 130 years. We should acknowledge that the natural order of living things is more peaceable than Darwin and his followers have thought; and we should spread a new conviction that we are behaving naturally when we behave peacefully.

When Darwin's bellicose philosophy led him to certain predictions, history had already proved him wrong. In 1871 he prophesied: "At some future period, not very distant as measured by centuries, the civilized races of man will almost certainly exterminate, and replace, the savage races throughout the world." What a strange concept of being civilized! Yet it seemed so "natural" at the time that it spread through the entire spectrum of intellectual activities. The beneficence of warfare enthralled imperialists as well as communists. Karl Marx, the apostle of class warfare, wanted to dedicate *Das Kapital* to Darwin. In 1860 he wrote to Engels: "Darwin's book is very important and serves me as basis in natural science for the class struggle in history."

The imperialists, in their heyday, made even freer use of the precepts of Social Darwinism. Karl Pearson, in his famous 1901 lecture "National Life from the Standpoint of Science," declared: "a nation is . . . an organized whole, kept up to a high pitch of internal efficiency by contest, chiefly by way of war with inferior races, and with equal races for trade-routes and the sources of raw material and of food supply. This is the natural history view of mankind."

It was a real tragedy, this strong feedback from imperialist thought patterns to biology—and vice versa. Darwin's original concept of evolution was so sound and necessary, so timely and all-embracing, that we can only wonder how it could prevail without acknowledging the driving force of cooperation and symbiosis.

Being deeply inhibited and straight-laced Victorians, nineteenth-century scientists could not admit the decisive role of Eros in the world. Imperialistic conquest was the order of the day, and it left its mark on biological theory.

Luckily, the past two decades have initiated a change of approach among many life-scientists. Fritjof Capra writes in his thought-provoking book *The Turning Point:*

Detailed study of ecosystems over the past decades has shown quite clearly that most relationships between living organisms are essentially cooperative ones, characterized by coexistence and interdependence, and symbiotic in various degrees. . . . This insight is in sharp contrast to the views of the Social Darwinists, who saw life exclusively in terms of competition, struggle, and destruction."[28]

John A. Wiens, a meticulous observer of small animals, comes to a similar conclusion: "The birds of grassland and shrubsteppe seem to be telling us that . . . Darwin's 'great battle of life' may be fought in skirmishes that are interspersed with periods of relative peace."[29]

And yet, this friendly view of nature has a hard time penetrating into the general thinking of most ethologists. Even a gentle, humanistic biologist like René Dubos writes: "Since most animals live by feeding on other creatures, killing is a biological necessity."[30] Hold it! Most animals feed on other creatures? The ancient dog-eats-dogma must indeed have nefarious power if an "objective" scientist can pronounce such a topsy-turvy statement!

By far the most numerous groups of mammals, such as rodents and hoofed animals, never touch meat. Carnivores like canines and felines comprise less than 1 percent of the mammalian population of any given habitat. Birds are a mixed crowd, some eat seeds and fruit, some insects; true birds of prey are a tiny minority. Among the reptiles, lizards and snakes are carnivorous, land turtles vegetarians. Fish—probably half and half. Among the arthropods, spiders, dragonflies, and wasps require other animals for their diets; bees, moths, and butterflies like only honey. It is perfectly obvious that very few animals live by feeding on other animals, and that combat, killing, and cruelty are rare phenomena. Just open your eyes on your next nature walk: how much killing do you see going on in forests and meadows? Do you see "unending struggle?" Or peace and beauty?

One question remains: Why should plant-eaters appear any more *simpatico* than meat-eaters? The answer must necessarily be subjective, but we can safely say that plants feel no pain (the opinion of some Indian biologists to the contrary). About 65 million years ago flowering plants and honey-sucking insects appeared simultaneously, and ever since their dependence on each other has amounted to symbiosis. Likewise, 25 million years ago grasses and hoofed animals spread together over several continents, depending on each other, always maintaining a loose equilibrium. Grass grows stronger by being cropped, and it becomes less of a fire hazard; it also profits from the ungulates' fertilizer.

I would go even further and say that certain seeds and fruits demand to be eaten—they are built that way, their only *raison d'être* is their edibility. No animal can be said to be created solely in order to be devoured, animals try to avoid a violent death. In contrast, the mistletoe can only propagate its species if its berries are swallowed by birds, transported into high trees, and deposited there with the birds' feces. The mistletoe simply has no other method of spreading its seeds; it would become extinct without hungry birds.

Another example is the truffle. This underground mushroom would seem to be a very impracticable apparatus, because all other mushrooms spread their spores with wind and rain. The buried truffle emits a strong, extremely attractive odor, which penetrates to the surface and attracts swine, goats, and, indirectly, gourmets. The truffle wants to be uprooted and eaten! It has no other way to distribute its spores than through feces. If the French peasants knew this fact, they would empty their chamber pots in their forests, truffles would become more numerous, and hence cheaper.

Meat-eaters have one more trait that makes them feared and, biosophically speaking, unsympathetic: In order to eat, they destroy each prey totally, including its future progeny. There is no nibbling off a limb, as there is with plant-eaters. Vegetarian animals eat those parts of a plant that can be regenerated: fruits, leaves, hardly ever roots. The percentage of mature plants killed for food must be far less than one in a million. Seedlings are destroyed in a much higher frequency range, but they are highly expandable and they don't feel pain.

Yet even in these matters, a law of compensation may be in force: carnivores need much smaller quantities of food than herbivores. A rattlesnake is satisfied with a dozen meals per year. Some sharks, too, seem to eat only once a month. The praying mantis catches one insect a day. Desert reptiles subsist on one insect in several days. Of course, this is not an absolute rule—frogs and toads eat all the time, and the tree shrew must hunt incessantly to eat the two-thirds of its own weight in food it requires each day. Furthermore, mammals have to invest ten times more energy than reptiles just to heat their bodies to around 37 degrees centigrade. Still, lions spend only a half hour of every second day dining, whereas the zebras around them eat during half their waking time.

On the whole, nature behaves in a surprisingly non-Darwinian, peaceable way.

For average, academic biologists, pain, fright, and despair of their "objects" are no concerns that would enter their laboratories and field studies. Objective natural science accords the same cool attention to the eating of plants and of animals. It never takes sides between predator and prey. And this is as it should be. Yet many non-academic questions involving nature and our own lives are waiting to be solved or at least pondered. What about the fear of death? The sense of life? Directional evolution? Free will? All these problems should indeed be treated by a life science; but anthropology, ethology, sociology, zoology, and the like have their well-circumscribed subjects.

We need a new discipline, a somewhat undisciplined discipline that dares to tackle the deepest riddles of life. Philosophy starts its work from ideas; modern biology takes its start from genes, biochemical processes, actions and reactions of organisms. Biosophy, starting at the juncture of these two endeavors, can transcend them both.

The biosopher can "feel" with the victims of aggression, be they animals or humans. He is not obliged to shy away from value-judgments. He can feel empathy with the caterpillar wriggling to avoid a bird's peak, as well as with the political prisoner subjected to sophisticated torture. For the biosopher, the withdrawal-reaction makes the difference: Plants cannot flee from a menace, most animals can. Where we can observe a flight-reaction, we can assume that there is fear. Grass and truffle don't mind being eaten, the rabbit does. Poets often understood the "timorous beastie," behaviorists never did. The flight-reaction is the great biosophical divide.

This also clarifies the concept of aggression in nature. The cow munching grass is not an aggressor, of course. How about a white blood corpuscle devouring a bacterium? We cannot judge without taking feelings into account. And this—the inclusion of sentiments and sense, directedness and purpose—defines biosophy.

All aggression in nature has to do with four quests: the quest for food, for sex, for dominance, or for territory.

The white blood corpuscle eating the bacterium would never destroy its territory. When a cell behaves in a manner that leads to the self-destruction of the entire system, we call it a cancer cell and we try to excise or subdue it.

Yet this is precisely what the human aggressive spirit has become: a cancer, spreading by means of an uncontrolled arms race and threatening to destroy humanity's territory, the planet Earth.

We have found that aggression in nature is mostly purposeful and short, and that most "wild" creatures have a peaceable life and a natural death. Thus our staggering load of armaments is completely unnatural.

The Soviets may have 20,000 atomic weapons, the United States perhaps 30,000. The latest Pentagon estimates are 26,000 U.S. warheads vs. 34,000 Soviet warheads. No matter. Two hundred such bombs would suffice to destroy the United States or the Soviet Union.

To freeze the level of arms now seems a modest proposal, a minimum which could be realized.

Freeze or fry.

Various models for the man of the future are being advertised. It does not seem so very long ago that the one-track development of a master race was propagated; the aim was a superman who would eradicate all pity within himself and all subhumans around him. Today *Homo technicus* is most often projected, sometimes with admiration, sometimes with loathing. The perfect technocrat is an extension of the earlier model of *Homo faber,* the mundane and productive man. The ruler of a thoroughly technicized world has received an aura of inevitability through brave-new-worldly science fiction. But his position in futuristic projections has been challenged by the opposite type, by *Homo contemplativus.* Meditation, concern for the rights of minorities, anti-war efforts are the symptoms of this ascending mentality. Will the upcoming generation be able to reconcile these opposites?

Technicized man seems to be lacking in antitoxins against the seductions of the military-industrial superiority complex. Contemplative man, on the other hand, is in danger of being drawn toward artificial paradises of drugs and illusions; he may disdain urgently needed practical reforms.

Which model of Homo sapiens has the best chance of being developed, short of cataclysmic final solutions?

There may be another type of future human being whose aims seem attainable and natural when we consider the profile of the species. May we call him "biosophical man"?

Johann Gottfried Herder wrote two centuries ago: "Man has no nobler word to designate his destiny than his own name."

Exactly. Being human anyway, we might as well enhance our "hominitude" more consciously. Man as a task is far from being fulfilled. In almost all Western languages the adjective denoting our humanity has a comparative and a superlative degree: *plus humain, menschlicher, il più umano,* more human. This is not a matter of course: Words like "froggier," or "the most flyish" would not make sense. The English language has developed the Latin root *humanus* into two branches: human and humane; yet both still are subsumed under the same concept. The half-conscious, autonomous spirit of the language has selected the milder qualities out of all the contradictory human characteristics. It has disregarded our potential for cruelty, vengefulness, power-madness, and it has decided that the attributes of care, altruism, temperance, peacefulness can best fill out the contour design of "the human being."

Our comparative and superlative aim should be: more humane, the most human—for life's sake. Since all life is directional, it is only fitting that we should think of ourselves as being on the way.

Summing Up:
An Optimist Manifesto

"I can fulfill three of your wishes," said the fairy to the little boy. His first two wishes were modest demands. But then the wish-child said: "My third wish is that you'll fulfill three wishes for me." And so on and on.

Homo sapiens has always vacillated between excessive self-esteem and depressive self-denial. Greek antiquity believed, with Protagoras, that "man was the measure of all things." Copernicus peeled away the protective onion-layers of the heavenly spheres surrounding us, until our egocentricity dissolved. Darwin finally abolished our special place apart from all other creatures. This devaluation makes the undertone of moody nihilism in modern life understandable: We lost the certainty of divine or fated purpose in our tasks and actions. We look up to the spiral nebulae and feel like negligible specks of dust. But this is really an erroneous perspective: with equal justification we could consider the atom and feel, in comparison, like godlike giants! A more realistic localization was prescribed by Pascal: Man holds the middle between nothingness and totality. To be the center from which we observe, judge and, if possible, improve the surrounding world: this is our natural position.

"The purpose of life is life itself," wrote Goethe. However, did Goethe's life not possess more purpose than, say, the existence of Sisyphus? How much sense is there to our lives if we happen not to be a Goethe? Would it be enough for everybody just to live for life's sake, without pursuing superimposed purposes? Would "life for life's sake" amount to an endless, vicious circle game? Not if life itself is a desirable good; not if it is directional.

Since most earlier aims that were felt to be obligatory—mystical, theological, provincial-patriotic aims—have proved to be disappointing, individuals today must make their own personal decisions as to purposes they want to accept. No sense is given automatically or decreed from above. Whenever a concrete endeavor seems to promote life, it is felt to be sensible. But is life constituted in such a way that we can regard it as the main factor in "making" sense? Is life worth all the trouble? What is life?

Many wise men—Democritos, Spencer, Nietzsche, Darwin—have told us that life is war or at least struggle, that the fittest should be victorious and should have the right to eliminate the weaker or gentler beings. This is a complete falsification of our traditional humane world view. More important, it is demonstrably untrue, and it does not take into consideration many observable facts. From the tiny mayfly—which lives only one day and sinks to its natural death uneaten (it is too small to stimulate any birds' voraciousness)—to the giant elephant who fulfills his physiologically given life span without being bothered by any enemies, there are innumerable creatures who never serve as food and who never persecute other animals. Ants (which make up more than half of the earth's population) are not eaten in any significant percentage.

True, the swallow flits all day through the atmosphere, snapping up thousands of living, suffering insects. This is caused by the fact that the air can't provide any protective mimicry in the daytime; for this reason those insects who want to live airborne have to overcompensate by enormous fertility. Thus they make the swallow possible in the first place. A cruel mechanism? Certainly. Wherever meat-eating is practiced, natural selection renders the meat-eater as efficient as possible. However: Only roughly one-twentieth of all animals are killed and eaten by carnivores.

The overwhelming majority dies a peaceful, "natural" death.

It is said that predators are necessary in order to eliminate the weak and malformed specimens and to improve the inheritable characteristics of all species. This, too, is only true to a very limited extent. The North American herds of buffalo lived peacefully through eons without being thinned out by raptorial foes, until the white man "improved" the balance of nature by almost exterminating the buffalo. The unmenaced fauna on islands, protected against the influx of predaceous animals, produces the most enchanting, gentle, and colorful life forms. Predators are not urgently needed!

Seen in purely biosophical terms, love is incomparably more important than combat and hatred.

Cooperation in nature is at least as frequent and as decisive as competition. We must only learn to see the superimposed units of life. A forest protects and supports its members: The mantle with its green branches extending down to the bottom is an organ comparable to our skin; it keeps out destructive storms and protects the interior against abrupt temperature changes and desiccation. Reed—a mass of many stalks, which is defined as singular by common usage—is really a unit: No single stem could defend itself against wind and rain. People have used this same principle consciously for breeding improved grains: A wheat field consists of individually helpless plants; each plant, trusting its cooperating sisters, can convert most of its energy into nourishing kernels instead of wasting it on a uselessly thick and strong stalk—thus drastically reducing its defense budget. Each such landscape unit is helpfulness made visible. A meadow wants to spread and preserve its health as a whole, it heals its wounds by overgrowing bald spots, it is an organism. Rethinking and restructuring the world in this holistic fashion, we arrive at more hopeful aims and purposes than were ever derived from the Darwinian idea that life is a struggle and nothing else.

If earthly existence amounted to war of all against all, the "fittest" surviving organisms, relying solely on mimicry, would have developed into camouflaged, prickly, gray, evil-smelling, bad-tasting, possibly poisonous creatures. We see no prevalence of these; instead, nature produces enticingly beautiful, colorful blossoms, butterflies, fish, birds. Why? Attraction—for fertilization, for the mere joy of life—is as important a principle as the dreary hide-and-seek of mimicry. Nature is not a stern, inexorable goddess. Not all conspicuous creatures are pounced upon and devoured. One well-known biologist said that "natural death is rather unnatural"! This does not hold true for the vast majority of creatures, both animal and human. Naturally it is natural to die a natural death!

The rise, development, and fall of species shows a certain whimsicality of nature, a loose play with strange and delightful formations. Many particular features, which seem to us of interest or aesthetic value, have no advantage that would warrant their selection for survival. The most beautiful forms—peacock, argus pheasant, hummingbird—cannot possibly be explained by "survival of the fittest;" they serve love, not war. "Survival of the fanciest" is a very frequent phenomenon. For most blossoms and butterflies, only the laws of aesthetic selection are operative: the more beautiful exemplars prefer each other and augment their charms by selective propagation through innumerable generations. The melodies of songbirds are not intended to drive away territorial competitors, otherwise they would have, by natural selection, turned into hissing, croaking, ugly sound utterance that would be more efficient by their very repugnance. The enhancement of lovely birdsongs serves the marital bond and the singer's own self-enjoyment. Life has an immanent tendency toward beautification.

Only homo sapiens has not yet joined this general improvement society. A strange, perverted conscience seems to prevent us from spreading enjoyment. Sometimes it appears that humankind alone wants to reverse the general trend toward beauty that is observable throughout the biosphere. Nature develops from drab lichens and horsetails to orchids and roses, from worms to butterflies, from tapir to horse. Human beings spread an ugly, unhealthy pall across the landscape. We put smoking factories, tacky suburbs, automobile graveyards where meadows and forests used to be. Only recently have we begun to criticize and stop the despoilment. William Blake demanded as early as in 1802 that the dark, satanic mills should give way to a new Jerusalem. Perhaps our awakened ecological conscience will now change the world for the better.

Progress and continuing refinement were very obvious in the

overall biological development. But how does our own species fit into this optimistic picture?

The history of homo sapiens was not always worthy of the designation "sapiens." Over vast stretches of time and space, very little productively oriented endeavor was discernable. The swelling and ebbing of tribes and dynasties inimical to one another, genocide and slaving expeditions, class struggle and religious persecutions: It is difficult to see any direction in this enormous unfolding of energy. But, first, it is not written that history must continue in the same vein. Second, we can abstract the bloody surface, we can look at deeper manifestations of the human spirit. And there we can discern an obvious direction. The improvement of knowledge and insight into natural phenomena, the incredibly complex accomplishments in technical and medical fields, the reproductive multiplication of works of art, literature, and music: It is impossible not to call all this progress. That we have not yet realized our ideals in political and social matters should not lead us into pessimistic resignation: More and more people seem at least to agree on ideals that are worth striving for.

Many taboos, inhibitions, and compulsions that opposed true progress are already in the process of dissolution. The acquisition of martial glory, for example, is no longer considered a worthy goal. The two proofs of masculinity—that a man had to be fruitful and frightful—used to cancel each other out and thus made possible two crude kinds of pleasurable entertainment. Today both games: the overproduction of babies and of corpses, having become much too risky, should be declared closed. Masculinity is not as important as "hominity."

We are able to deflect and redirect our noxious drives toward new aims. For this we possess a marvelous tool: the brain. The human spirit has an absolutely unique position in nature: It is the only agent that can move from nearby atoms to spiral nebulae and back with speeds faster than light. Through the leverage of projection, we can influence things incomparably more efficiently than our soft, relatively weak, easily wounded physiques seem to warrant. Human thought by itself, inside the skull, has no strength, no motion; but transformed into planning and organizing, it becomes most powerful. Consequently, the efficiency of the intellect in many concerns has no bounds. Why should we not, finally, utilize it to digest and redirect our inherited Neanderthal drives?

We human beings are capable of changing ourselves in several basic ways, through the process of learning, to our own and the biosphere's advantage. Learning is our instrument for adapting to the technicized world whose modifications, originally caused by us, are now part and parcel of nature. Learning is, of course, more than data compilation and complication; it changes our character. It is the continuation, sped-up and purpose-oriented, of the progressive development which has dominated the animal kingdom for eons already and which brought forth ever new, more efficient, more intelligent, and also more beautiful forms.

Life as such has four immanent vectors (or, put a little too anthropomorphically, intentions): Life wants to preserve itself, it wants to spread, it wants to satisfy itself, and it wants to refine itself.

This fourfold path of life has made the surface of this planet more viable and more agreeable for higher-organized beings. It certainly was not a straight development; stagnation and setbacks occurred again and again. But there was plenty of time. As a result, the biosphere became subtler and more beautiful. Algae turned into apple trees, worms were transmuted into peacocks. Humankind, which began as a small particle of the biosphere, inherited an earth that became more hospitable in the same measure as the race became more expansive.

As natural beings, we carry the four vectors of life within ourselves: self-preservation, spreading, drive toward satisfaction, and ever-growing refinement. If these four forces can be integrated to serve and enhance life—all life on earth—then the future will be open to us.

Through learning, we can acquire an indeterminate number of new characteristics that we will, through the cultural process, pass on from generation to generation. A precarious, but indispensable endowment! Our inventory of inherited qualities is exactly circumscribed, but the number of acquired reactions and actions is unlimited and unlimitable. This is the main advantage learning has over purely biological development.

Yet the civilizing process is no less natural than the preceding development through natural selection. Theoretically, the strict separation between biological and cultural processes has the undesirable effect of making nature and culture appear as opposites. They are, however, both part of a single, directional process. Our very bodies depend on the products of civilization and on cultured thinking. Contrary to all other animals, we cannot bend down toward the surface of a creek or waterhole in order to drink; thus we need a vessel. When our ancestors climbed down out of the monkey tree and roamed the plains on two legs, their anatomies remained unbalanced; it was impossible to use the short arms for tasks of the soil while standing upright. To compensate, the stick was adapted for digging, as a weapon, and as a third leg for the infirm. The idea of the "useful thing," soon formalized into the tool, was caused physiologically—and that means, naturally. The use of a variety of tools and artifices, then, had its retro-effect on natural selection—we simply did not need prolongated arms, neck, or snout; there was no selective pressure to develop canine saber teeth, claws, hairy, leathery skin, or horny armor. Culture is not a foreign addition, it is an integral part of our existence.

"Back to nature"? This ideal makes sense only if it does not mean "back to our original Neanderthal nature."

The mounting complication culture brings with it—and which sometimes makes us sigh with discouragement—is not a devaluation, it is an augmentation of the general trend among living things: Nature also began with the simplest forms and led to multifarious, complicated organisms. Of course, all people should be able to take an occasional vacation to shed the compulsive mechanization for a few weeks. No insoluble problem there!

In order to deal with the future, we have free will at our disposal. It is certainly wrong to conceive of human beings as programmed mechanisms with only one fate. We can choose. Every day we make many decisions. It is not the motives that cause a certain action; it is the person whose psyche contains these motives who is the cause and originator of the act. Closed systems, such as automated factories and ocean steamers, can be steered for a long while by automatic robot pilots; but a sailboat, which must react constantly to unpredictable environmental influences, depends on a human will that can produce decisions. What purpose would a captain have if he had no free will?

The "I" stands between mental images of certain aims and activates the one that is most appealing: The aim is the cause of the action; finality and causality are only two aspects of the same effect. The ancient scholastic dilemma of Buridan's ass is simply not applicable to our everyday reality. No asinine or human being would be paralyzed by indecision between equal attractions.

It is not only the external causes that determine the choice between two possible modes of action. The "I" is plugged into the circuit each time, and that means that the person—including all experiences, theories, judgments, particular tastes, and motives— makes the decision.

Ergo, we are free. The pall of determinacy is taken from us, our fate is, to a larger or smaller extent, given into our own hands. Thus we have "cause" to consider life a desirable good. This makes possible an incredible elasticity of endeavor, an almost limitless richness of life.

We don't know how long life has already existed on earth. A few years ago, scientists were content with 500 million years. Recent estimates concerning the age of fossil algae go to 2 or 3 billion years. Surely our retrospect will become clearer as time goes on. And our prospect? How long shall life obtain its will on this planet?

We can pose the question even while knowing that there is no answer. One fact we do know: The spark of life, which started in unthinkably early times, has never again stopped glowing. Like the Olympic torch it is passed on from one organism to the next. Doesn't this put a high obligation on us?

It does not suffice that we send fertile sex cells out into the unknown, dark stream of the future. We also must deed the will to live to our descendants—a difficult task in an epoch of far-reaching discouragement.

These decades may actually be the most dangerous in the world's history, the tight passage in the hourglass. Overpopulation, the unjust and inefficient distribution of wealth, the possibility of nuclear war: Everyone is aware of these three terrible menaces. Some of the problems are technical and can be solved by men and women of good will who combine the best features of *Homo technicus* and *Homo contemplativus*. Since we possess *free will,* we can also organize *good will.*

If wisdom can manage to tame the ancient instincts of combativeness and unchecked fertility, life will have a chance to prevail —if not for billions, at least for a few hundred thousand of years; we don't want to be greedy, after all. Then life will be able to spread, refine, and beautify itself and to seek its little and big satisfactions. We have to pass through the bottleneck of present miseries and dangers, to protect and care for the spark, to preserve life for life's sake.

Notes

1. Edward O. Wilson, *On Human Nature* (Cambridge, Mass.: Harvard University Press, 1978), p. 99.
2. Robert Ardrey, *African Genesis* (London: Collins, 1961), p. 316.
3. G. A. M. King, "Symbiosis and the Origin of Life," *Origins of Life* 8 (1977), p. 52.
4. George B. Schaller, *Serengeti* (New York: Knopf, 1972), pp. 11, 44, 81.
5. Sally Carrighar, *Wild Heritage* (Boston: Houghton Mifflin, 1965).
6. Charles Darwin, *The Origin of Species*, 1859.
7. Garret Hardin, *Biology* (San Francisco: W. H. Freeman, 1966), p. 242.
8. Konrad Lorenz, *On Aggression* (New York: Bantam, 1966), p. 20.
9. Teilhard de Chardin, *La Vision du Passé*, lecture in Peking, 1942; *The Phenomenon of Man* (New York, 1959).
10. Theodosius Dobzhansky, *Mankind Evolving* (Yale University Press, 1962), p. 215.
11. Isaac Asimov, *The Wellsprings of Life* (London: Abelard-Schuman, 1960), p. 48.
12. Franz Hančar, *Das Pferd* (Vienna, 1955).
13. Lorenz, *On Aggression*, p. 36.
14. Ibid., p. 157.
15. Mary Batten, "Sexual Olympics," *Science Digest* (December 1982), p. 82.
16. Ibid., p. 85.
17. Ibid., p. 83.
18. Lorenz, *On Aggression*, p. 38.
19. Ibid., p. 157.
20. Julian Huxley, *Evolution in Action* (New York: Harpers & Brothers, 1953), p. 63.
21. Einhard, *The Life of Charlemagne* (Ann Arbor: University of Michigan Press, 1960), p. 60.
22. Peter Kropotkin, *Ethics* (New York: Mac Veagh, 1924).
23. Dean E. Wooldridge, *Mechanical Man* (New York: McGraw-Hill, 1968), p. 183.
24. Ibid., p. 187.
25. David Hume, *An Enquiry Concerning Human Understanding* (1748).
26. B. F. Skinner, *Science and Human Behavior* (New York: Macmillan, 1953), p. 6.
27. Alfred North Whitehead, *The Function of Reason* (Princeton University Press, 1929; Beacon paperback, 1967), p. 16.
28. Fritjof Capra, *The Turning Point* (New York: Simon & Schuster, 1982), p. 279.
29. John A. Wiens, "Competition or Peaceful Coexistence?" *Natural History* (March 1981), p. 30.
30. René Dubos, *Beast or Angel?* (New York: Charles Scribner's Sons, 1974).